Her Secret Garden

A Daily Walk with Jesus

Laura Kringle

Kringle Publishers
Brunswick, Nebraska

Her Secret Garden: A Daily Walk with Jesus

Cover design copyright ©SelfPubBookCovers.com/RLSather

Logo by logomakr.com/7xFHZ6

Published by Kringle Publishers
Brunswick, NE
laurakringle87@gmail.com

Printed in the United States of America.

ISBN 978-1-7361153-0-5

Introduction

  While still in college, the Lord impressed upon my heart that one day I would write a women's devotional. Many years later, while compiling writings from my journals, the Lord let me know that I was to present the journal entries in chronological order as a devotional. He also said, **"It's a love story, little one. It's a love story between you and Me. I want you to publish this story and let others know the relationship they can have with their God, if they will but come."**

  And so I give to you some of what was given to me through the years. Some of the writings are the **Lord's own words** spoken in my spirit. **These are in bold print**. Others are ideas, poems, or stories I felt He inspired as I walked with Him through life.

  The scripture references at the end of each journal entry are meant to lead the reader into personal Bible study. It is my desire that those of you who read this devotional will take the time to look up the verses and delight in what God would share with you through His word.

  May this devotional encourage you in your own personal walk with the Lord. May it encourage you to spend time in the presence of the One who loves you.

Blessings,
Laura

Her Secret Garden

Oft she'd wander to her garden when she wanted time alone,
And she'd wave aside the ivy till her eyes fell on the stone.
Seeking entrance by a doorway that was hidden from all view,
Grasping then the golden handle, she would gracefully glide through.

There beneath the weeping willow or in other lovely spots,
She would rest with book in arbor or delight in numerous thoughts.
In the peace of all her moments she would lift her heart in prayer,
Thanking God for all His goodness, thanking God for all His care.

Oh, her garden was an armchair in the haven of her room.
It was there she found a refuge; it was there her peace would bloom.
For it was really in the Spirit that she found her place of rest,
In the loving arms of Jesus as she lay upon His breast.

– Laura Kringle
(1/2000)

January 1

(Journal 6-19-1982)
Lord, I *love* to be in Your presence!

"My dear child, I love to be in your presence as much as you love to be in Mine. If it were not so, I would not have died for you. For in dying, I brought you into My presence."

Colossians 1:22 (NLT) Yet now he has reconciled you to himself through the death of Christ in his physical body. As a result, he has brought you into his own presence, and you are holy and blameless as you stand before him without a single fault.

Ephesians 2:13
Psalm 147:11

January 2

(Journal 10-13-1982)
I once asked Jesus how I could show my love for Him. (It's one thing to say it, but another thing to show it.)
He answered, **"By loving others."**
I forget so often—it should be so clear—whatever we have done unto the least of one of His brothers, we have done to Him (Matt. 25:40).

Hebrews 6:10 (NLT) For God is not unjust. He will not forget how hard you have worked for him and how you have shown your love to him by caring for other believers, as you still do.
1 John 5:1-3
John 15:12

January 3

(Journal 12-21-1982)
I was pouring out my frustrations to the Lord tonight, wondering when I was going to be put to service. I was feeling like my time and my life were being wasted. Though I was reading a lot of scripture, and listening to tapes, I felt even *that* could be a waste of time if I did nothing, and had nothing to show for it.

Then He said, **"A vessel that the potter is not yet finished with will leak. It will lose that which is put into it."**

Here, I interrupted Him, because I had a pottery class in high school and I couldn't see how, if you poured water into a clay pot that was on the potter's wheel, it would leak out.

He said**, "The clay is so soft that any little bruise will cause a hole, and the contents will be lost."** Then He caused me to think about how, in our lives, we are always open to bruises.

He continued, **"The vessel needs to be fired to make it strong and fit for use."**

It is often shown in the Bible how we are tested by fire.

I am so impatient. I need to pray again for patience, although that too will come in time. We want to take our lives into our own hands, forgetting that He is the Potter, our Maker, and we are only the vessel.

He wants to fill me with His Spirit, with power, with His gifts, but until this vessel is ready, that which is put into it will only be lost—wasted.

Isaiah 45:9-12 (NLT) "What sorrow awaits those who argue with their Creator. Does a clay pot argue with its maker? Does the clay dispute with the one who shapes it, saying, 'Stop, you're doing it wrong!' Does the pot exclaim, 'How clumsy can you be?' How terrible it would be if a newborn baby said to its father, 'Why was I born?' or if it said to its mother, 'Why did you make me this way?'" This is what the Lord says—the Holy One of Israel and your Creator: "Do you question what I do for my children? Do you give me orders about the work of my hands? I am the one who made the earth and created people to live on it. With my hands I stretched out the heavens. All the stars are at my command."

Isaiah 64:8
Romans 9:20-21
Isaiah 48:10

January 4

(Journal 3-11-1983)
"Never turn your foot from following the path I have laid out for you.

Know that the life I've called you to will be a life of sacrifice, a life of labor, a life of pain. Know that I have called you to share in the glory as well as the labor; that the rewards at the end are great.

My children shall not be disappointed. Those who love their life shall lose it, but those who lose their life for My sake shall find it."

Isaiah 48:17 (NLT) This is what the LORD says—your Redeemer, the Holy One of Israel: "I am the LORD your God, who teaches you what is good for you and leads you along the paths you should follow."

Acts 14:22
Luke 6:22-23
Mark 8:34-38

January 5

(Journal 3-14-1983)
    What has been missing from my life is thanksgiving for all things. The moment I started thanking God for everything, even the seemingly bad things, my heart was flooded with joy and God's presence became very near.

Ephesians 5:20 (NIV) ...always giving thanks to God the Father *for* everything, in the name of our Lord Jesus Christ.

1 Thessalonians 5:16-18
Job 2:10
Psalm 69:30-31

January 6

(Journal 2-5-1984)
    I was allowing a woman I take care of at the nursing home to change my attitude to one of bitterness because of her unkindness toward me and toward all those she came in contact with. The Lord reminded me of Romans 12:21 "Do not be overcome by evil, but overcome evil with good." Praise be to God, my attitude toward her changed and I was able to love her no matter what she said.
    The last day I took care of her, she was steaming over an injustice done toward her by another. While she was claiming to be a Christian, she was letting unforgiveness destroy her. I patted her hand and said, "The best thing we can do for them is to pray for them and forgive them." She angrily said, "You always bring that up!" I reminded her of the verse

that says, "Love your enemies, bless those that curse you, pray for those who despitefully use you." "Humph, I don't believe it!" I then said, "If you are a Christian, you will believe what Jesus said, and he told us to love and forgive others." "Oh just shut up!" She bitterly retorted. But later on that day I noticed a change in her—she smiled, and said, "Thank you," to me for the second time ever, and she greeted each resident she passed as I wheeled her to the activities department. Near the end of the day, she kissed me on the cheek and said, "I love you."

Matthew 6:14-15 (NLT) "If you forgive those who sin against you, your heavenly Father will forgive you. But if you refuse to forgive others, your Father will not forgive your sins."

Proverbs 28:23 (NKJV) He who rebukes a man will find more favor afterward than he who flatters with the tongue.

Luke 6:27-28

January 7

(Journal 4-12-1984)

It was suddenly clear to me this morning that the road the Good Samaritan traveled was the road of life. In a vision, I saw myself traveling this road, passing by many who were wounded, and I did not stop to help.

I had often thought that if I saw someone lying hurt on the road I would most certainly stop to help and would not pass to the other side as the men in the story had done. But I am guilty with them when I think of those whom I have walked right past, closing my eyes to their hurts and problems—not wanting to get involved.

"Father, forgive me! Let me see the needs, and as I see, let me act." The Good Samaritan did something about what he saw. His concern was expressed not only in words, but in action.

Galatians 6:1-3 (NLT) Dear brothers and sisters, if another believer is overcome by some sin, you who are godly should gently and humbly help that person back onto the right path. And be careful not to fall into the same temptation yourself. Share each other's burdens, and in this way you obey the law of Christ.

Luke 10:30-37
1 John 3:16-23

January 8

(Journal 4-18-1984)

    This afternoon I prayed, "Lord, I want You to take full rein in my life." In my spirit I heard, **"Do you really mean that? I can't take half the rein while you have the other half, for I would be pulling one way and you would be pulling another, and we'd be pulling against each other."**

    "Lord, help me to give You complete rein. Lead me in the way that I should go."

Romans 8:14 (NIV) ...because those who are led by the Spirit of God are sons of God.

Psalm 31:3
Psalm 139:24

January 9

(Journal 8-7-1984)
"Where are the quiet moments in your life, when I might speak to you?

My precious child, I will never leave you alone. You have given your life to Me, will I cast it away? My eyes are upon you always.

Hold fast that which I have taught you. Hold fast the truths of My word.

To those who believe are the treasures of My fellowship.

Lie in quiet and know that I Am God."

Psalm 46:10 (NIV) "Be still, and know that I am God..."
Hebrews 13:5b
Psalm 34:15
Proverbs 4:13

January 10

(Journal 8-8-1984)
A prayer concerning my Junior High Wednesday night class:

"Father, tonight I felt their minds were not on the class."

"You did not do battle against the enemy for their ears:
- Claim their ears and hearts for Jesus.
- Rest assured that I will answer your prayer.
- Offer the sacrifice of thanksgiving."

Ephesians 6:12 (NKJV) For we do not wrestle against flesh and blood, but against principalities, against powers, against the rulers of the darkness of this age, against spiritual hosts of wickedness in the heavenly places.

1 John 5:14-15
Philippians 4:6

January 11

(Journal 6-29-1985)
>   **"Allow Me to minister to and through you. Are you not thankful when I speak to you through another? In the same way, allow Me to speak to another through you. Be that vessel through which My love may pass to another in need."**

1 Peter 4:10-11 (NIV) Each one should use whatever gift he has received to serve others, faithfully administering God's grace in its various forms. If anyone speaks, he should do it as one speaking the very words of God. If anyone serves, he should do it with the strength God provides, so that in all things God may be praised through Jesus Christ. To him be the glory and the power for ever and ever. Amen.

1 Thessalonians 5:11
2 Corinthians 7:5-7

January 12

(Journal 7-1-1985)
   "If you only knew, little one, what you were missing; if you only knew the spiritual blessings I have to give you, you would be the first one up every morning, waiting at the feet of your Lord. Come, taste, see that the Lord is good. Don't stand apart in the cold when there is fellowship, warm and real, so close at hand."

   "Oh, Father, help me to draw nearer to You, that You might draw nearer to me. For this is my heart's desire."

Psalm 5:3 (NIV) In the morning, O LORD, you hear my voice; in the morning I lay my requests before you and wait in expectation.

Psalm 119:147
Psalm 34:8

January 13

(Journal 7-2-1985)
   Yesterday, while setting tables in the dining room at the Summer Institute of Linguistics, I saw a little boy waddling after his mom, while he held a cup in his left hand. Suddenly, his feet slipped out from under him and he fell to the floor. My heart leapt inside and I was filled with love and compassion for the little guy. I picked up the crying little boy and set him on his feet again. Soon, his mom was at his side.
   As I continued to set tables, I heard the Lord say, **"Do you think I love you any less than the love you felt for that little boy when you saw him fall?"**

How much more love *He* must have for us when He sees His little ones fall. I started crying just thinking of His love.

Psalm 145:13b-14 (NIV) The LORD is faithful to all his promises and loving toward all he has made. The LORD upholds all those who fall and lifts up all who are bowed down.

Proverbs 24:16

January 14

(Journal 9-9-1985)
    "My Child, if you take the time to meet with Me each morning, you will not be disappointed. My children that meet with Me find new strength to face the day, new courage to replace the old."
    The Lord impressed on me to remember the illustration of the manna—'gather afresh each morning', from Exodus 16:21.

Psalm 29:11 (NKJV) The LORD will give strength to His people; the LORD will bless His people with peace.

Isaiah 33:2
Exodus 16:4
John 6:57-58

January 15

(Journal 10-29-1985)
"...I pray just as much, but it's our relationship that changes. I don't take the time to bask in Your presence—to sit at Your feet. I'm too busy, like Martha, trying to get everything done—to get everyone prayed for. I don't take the time to just enjoy who You are, to thrill at my established position as a child of God."

When I have taken the time to *'come away to a quiet place and rest awhile'* (Mark 6:31), I can go back to the *work* refreshed and motivated. Martha was busy *serving* the Lord, but Mary took the time to first sit at the feet of Jesus.

The characteristic of those who don't take the time to sit at the feet of Jesus is 'anxiety.' "Martha, Martha, thou art anxious and upset about many things" (Luke 10:41).

How true I have found this in my own life. The peace that I have when I sit at the feet of Jesus is beautiful.

Matthew 11:28-30 (NIV) "Come to me, all you who are weary and burdened, and I will give you rest. Take my yoke upon you and learn from me, for I am gentle and humble in heart, and you will find rest for your souls. For my yoke is easy and my burden is light."

Psalm 23:2-3a (NIV) He makes me lie down in green pastures, he leads me beside quiet waters, he restores my soul.

Luke 10:38-42

January 16

(Journal 11-27-1985)
Praise the Lord! Last night, around 6:30, I prayed for one of my patients at the nursing home. Yesterday, she told me that she had been treated unkindly the evening before. So I

prayed that others would treat her more kindly, and that the Lord would wrap His loving arms around her. The Lord's compassion for her fell from my eyes as I prayed.

This morning she said the girl that took care of her last night hugged her, kissed her and told her that she loved her. When she said this, I remembered my prayer and thanked the Lord.

The Lord is truly watching out for her in a special way.

Ephesians 4:32 (NIV) Be kind and compassionate to one another...

Psalm 34:15
Psalm 146:5-9

January 17

(Journal 12-18-1985)

I walked up the stairs tonight after dinner feeling mentally and physically exhausted. I thought about the Bible study I needed to lead with the youth that night. As I sat on the edge of my bed and told the Lord how I was feeling, 'August 25th' in the book *God Calling*, flashed through my mind. I looked it up, and afterward thanked the Lord. He is so good!

Here is what I read:

Exhaustion - August 25th

We seek Thee as Thou hast told us.

And seeking you shall find. None ever sought My Presence in vain. None ever sought My Help in vain. A breath of desire and My Spirit is there—to replenish and renew. Sometimes weariness and exhaustion are not signs of lack of spirit but of the guiding of the Spirit. Many wonderful things would not have happened but for the physical weariness, the mind-weariness of My servants, which made the resting apart, the giving up of work a necessity... Though My Way may seem a narrow way it yet leads to Life, abundant Life. Follow it. It is not so narrow but that I can tread it beside you. Never too lonely with such companionship. A comrade infinitely tender, infinitely strong, will tread the way with you.

Isaiah 40:28-31 (NKJV) Have you not known? Have you not heard? The everlasting God, the LORD, the Creator of the ends of the earth, neither faints nor is weary. His understanding is unsearchable. He gives power to the weak, and to those who have no might He increases strength. Even the youths shall faint and be weary, and the young men shall utterly fall, but those who wait on the LORD shall renew their strength; they shall mount up with wings like eagles, they shall run and not be weary, they shall walk and not faint.

God Calling, Edited by A. J. Russell,
Berkley Publishing Group, 1978

January 18

(Journal 12-27-1985)
"Oh, My precious one, to you does My voice call. To you do I reach out in love. Can you not hear? Can you not see? Daily, My blessings are upon you. Daily, I shower you with My love.

Look to Me for strength and guidance. My hand is ever before you, leading you in the way that you should go. Take it and walk with Me, little one.

Find protection in the One who is able to drive a demon to its knees. Find strength in the One who makes a mountain to bow."

Psalm 42:8 (NLT) But each day the LORD pours his unfailing love upon me, and through each night I sing his songs, praying to God who gives me life.

Psalm 5:7-8
Isaiah 48:17
2 Thessalonians 3:3

January 19

(Journal 1-27-1986)
    "My little one, I would correct you with an arm of love. Look to Me to supply your needs. For a Father I am, and what father would not meet the needs of a child he loved, who cried to him for that which he all along desired to give him. When once that child turns to see its value, will the Father not leap immediately and bestow upon him this gift? Look to Me, little one. I shall supply your needs."

Philippians 4:19 (NKJV) And my God shall supply all your need according to His riches in glory by Christ Jesus.

John 16:27 (NKJV) "...for the Father Himself loves you,"

Matthew 6:8 (NLT) "...for your Father knows exactly what you need even before you ask him!"

January 20

(Journal 1-29-1986)
    We are but simple instruments.

"Simple instruments in the hands of a Mighty God can be used mightily."

1 Chronicles 11:9 (NLT) And David became more and more powerful, because the LORD of Heaven's Armies was with him.

1 Samuel 17:40-50
1 Chronicles 29:10-13

January 21

(Journal 2-1-1986)

While cleaning out one of my drawers tonight, I came across something I wrote in the Spring:

"As I was looking out the window this evening at the beauty of Spring, the Lord spoke into my heart, saying, **'All of this is yours.'** My concept of something belonging to me meant I could grasp it in my hands. But for the first time, I understood this thought—though I could not hold the fluttering little humming bird in my hands, it belonged to me. For all things on this earth that belong to God, He has given to His children."

Psalm 115:16 (NKJV) The heaven, even the heavens, are the LORD'S; but the earth He has given to the children of men.

1 Corinthians 3:21-23

January 22

(Journal 2-28-1986)

"My Child, when a heart is still before Me and its ears listening to what I would speak, then shall it find joy and satisfaction to its heart's content. Spend time with Me. Spend time in My presence. Delight in Me. Delight to obey My word and your joy will be full.

Listen to the voice of your Father, for each day do I cry unto My children to hear and obey. Each day do I send My love. Each day do I renew My strength unto them, if they would but listen and believe. Strong is the Lord toward those that are weak.

Lift up your voice in praise, for then shall your heart be lifted up in joy. Let your faithfulness be renewed toward the God of your salvation. Come before My presence with singing. Be joyful in heart as you sing praise unto Me."

Psalm 89:15-17 (NLT) Happy are those who hear the joyful call to worship, for they will walk in the light of your presence, LORD. They rejoice all day long in your wonderful reputation. They exult in your righteousness. You are their glorious strength.

Psalm 9:1-2
Psalm 42:8
Psalm 119:17-18

January 23

(Journal 3-8-1986)

While interacting with one of my patients at the nursing home, self-pity clamored, "I don't deserve to be treated like this." And then I heard in my spirit, **"And neither did our**

Lord deserve to wear a crown of thorns. Neither did He deserve to be beaten, bruised and torn."

Isaiah 53
Psalm 44:13-22

January 24

(Journal 3-13-1986)

The Lord is so precious. Last Friday, I prayed about my Sunday school preparation. A short while later I turned on the radio to hear a woman discussing the *exact* story my lesson was to be based on. It was the story of Jairus seeking Jesus' help in the healing of his little daughter, and the woman that was healed after touching the hem of Jesus' garment.

The woman on the radio said she read this story as if she were reading it to Jesus. Luke 9:40, "At Your return, the crowd welcomed You, for they were looking for You. And a man named Jairus, a ruler of the synagogue, came and fell at Your feet and requested You to come to his house..."

I did this as I prepared the lesson, and oh, how it made the story come to life!

During Sunday school I didn't use the lesson book at all, but told the story just as I had visualized it happening.

"When I see Your love and guidance in little things like this, Jesus, it makes me all the more confident that You will help me in all things."

2 Chronicles 26:5 (NIV) He sought God during the days of Zechariah, who instructed him in the fear of God. As long as he sought the LORD, God gave him success.

Isaiah 41:13

January 25

(Journal 3-24-1986)
"My little one,

My precious little one, if you knew how much I loved you, you would not doubt My leading. You would rejoice and be glad."

Ephesians 3:16-21
Psalm 31:7a (NIV) I will be glad and rejoice in your love,...

January 26

(Journal 4-4-1986)
"I have never promised to obey Your word, for fear that I would not keep this promise and bring disgrace upon myself and bring Your wrath upon me also. But a man and a woman united in marriage make these vows: 'I promise to love, honor and obey...'

By Your strength and not my own, help me to keep this promise before You:

On this day of April 4, 1986, I promise to obey the word of truth, to seek and love the Lord with all my heart, to love my family, friends, neighbors and enemies as Christ loved the Church, to establish my foot firmly on the Rock of my salvation, to serve You with all my heart.

To do this, I commit myself before Jesus Christ, Savior and Lord, and before God the Father. Amen"

"Oh Lord, let me establish this promise within my heart forever, and let me not take it lightly. This day I have made this promise before You. Renew my life in You. Replenish my strength, open my hand and my heart to hear and understand. Keep my foot from slipping and my tongue from speaking evil. Fill me with the knowledge of Your grace, with an understanding of Your great love to all mankind. Let Your love dwell richly in my heart. Let my lips proclaim Your praise.

Heal the land. Heal this heart, O Lord, and let it produce fruit once again. Bring the healing winds of the south to blow upon this garden and spread the fragrance throughout."

"My little one, your words have reached My ears and My hand will be quick to respond. For I have seen your tears and know that now your heart toward Me is perfect. And as you obey My words, in Me will you find strength and great joy. Do not let your heart stray again from that which is good and right."

Psalm 119:57-58 (NIV) You are my portion, O LORD; I have promised to obey your words. I have sought your face with all my heart; be gracious to me according to your promise.

2 Chronicles 16:9
2 Chronicles 7:14

January 27

(Journal 12-13-1986)
"I want to bring everything to You like Sandy does."

"My little one, oh, that you would bring everything to Me like you used to do. Then would you find comfort for your soul in abundance. Then would the sun rise and not set within your soul. For there would be continual light, and daily would that light grow stronger."

Proverbs 4:18 (NIV) The path of the righteous is like the first gleam of dawn, shining ever brighter till the full light of day.

2 Corinthians 1:3-4

January 28

(Journal 3-20-1987)
What I heard upon waking:

"My little one, I would touch you with golden sunlight if the sun was near your head. I would bathe you with winds of morning if the wind was by your side. My love is expressed to My children in so many ways."

Psalm 143:8 (NIV) Let the morning bring me word of your unfailing love, for I have put my trust in you.

Psalm 139:17-18

January 29

(Journal 3-20-1987)
A few weeks ago, as I bent to get something out of my closet, I sat too near the corner of my bed and ripped my light blue corduroy pants. I threw them in the wastebasket because they were beyond repair.

My college roommate, said, "Laura, your poor pants. Doesn't it bother you? I would feel terrible!" I laughed and said, "I've learned not to set my heart upon the things I have.

The Lord taught me that, years ago, when all of my favorite things became ruined or lost. I got paint on my favorite jumper, lost my favorite earrings...the Lord knows that I don't have very many pairs of pants. I only have three pairs left, but He allowed it to happen. Besides, whenever I put those on I felt they looked a bit too tight."

My roommate looked at me and said, "Well, if nothing else, *I* learned something."

A few days ago, I was in Kmart with my sister and found a pair of light blue corduroy pants, very similar in appearance to the ones I had ripped. And praise the Lord, they were on sale for $3.00. I was amazed. They were marked down from $19.00 to $3.00! Kmart was getting rid of their winter clothes. Of all the clothes on a little circular rack, there were only one pair of pants in my size and they happened to be nearly identical to the ones I'd lost. When I tried them on, they fit perfectly; not as tight as my other pair. I kept thanking my Father for them.

Colossians 3:2 (NIV) Set your minds on things above, not on earthly things.

Matthew 6:28-33
Matthew 6:8

January 30

(Journal 3-28-1987)

"My little one, I have led you in so many ways. I will not stop now. My heart rejoices to see you in obedience; to see that your heart is tender toward Me, toward My voice, as I speak My desires for your life.

Come away, little one, to a quiet place. Learn of Me. Learn of My love. Refresh your soul in the springs of life. Renew your faith like that of a child's.

Communion with Me brings faith immeasurable, joy beyond bounds, love beyond limits.

My little one, I love you. I would that you would know the joys awaiting you, the pleasures I reserve for those who are obedient."

Hebrews 5:8-9 (NKJV) ...though He was a Son, yet He learned obedience by the things which He suffered. And having been perfected, He became the author of eternal salvation to all who obey Him.

John 15:10
Mark 6:31
Psalm 16:11

January 31

(Journal 5-3-1987)

"I love you, My child. Know that I am with you. Know that I care. Know that I have given you a promise and will fulfill it.

Silence your heart before Me, that you may often hear the words that I would use to encourage you."

Matthew 28:20b (NKJV) "...and lo, I am with you always, even to the end of the age."

2 Corinthians 1:20
Psalm 131:2

**"I am a Friend,
To those who seek a friend.
I am a Supplier,
To those who seek a supplier.
Seek, and ye shall find."**

"Lord, when your sunshine is inside of me
then all the grey skies in the world
don't matter."

Complaining gives the glory to Satan,
but praising gives the glory to God.

February 1

(Journal 1-22-1988)
 "Draw near, My child, for I wish to show you so many things. My heart yearns to draw you into My treasury house of wisdom. There, understanding is dished out on an open palm. Receive freely, My child, receive freely."

"Father, let me make this time priority."

 "I would desire for you to do this, child. For only then will you be effective."

Proverbs 2:1-7a (NKJV) My son, if you receive my words, and treasure my commands within you, so that you incline your ear to wisdom, and apply your heart to understanding; Yes, if you cry out for discernment, and lift up your voice for understanding, if you seek her as silver, and search for her as for hidden treasures; then you will understand the fear of the LORD, and find the knowledge of God. For the LORD gives wisdom; from His mouth come knowledge and understanding; He stores up sound wisdom for the upright...

Job 28:28
Colossians 2:2-3

February 2

(Journal 2-18-1988)
 "I love you, little one, and My hand is upon you though you do not always see it or feel it. Know that I am swift to guide, swift to sustain, swift to draw My children ever nearer. And now would I draw you nearer to My breast and tenderly hold you as a mother holds her child.

Now, let your heart be swift to receive, swift to hear, swift to give."

Isaiah 66:13 (NIV) "As a mother comforts her child, so will I comfort you..."

Ezra 7:6
Ezra 8:31
James 1:19

February 3

(Journal 3-2-1988)

"My husband has said and done so many kind things to me, Father. Help me to remember to take the time to record so that I might not forget. I want to have good memories of him for the years when memories are all I will have. Help me to love him, Father."

This morning, John talked of learning to appreciate and love each other more. I said, part jokingly, "I've already learned that lesson, what's the next one?" But now as I pray, my heart convinces me I have *so much* to learn about loving and appreciating him. So often my love and appreciation is silently entertained within my own thoughts.

"Father, help me to be more verbal, more expressive."

I also question, "Am I meeting *his* needs? Do I even know what they are?"

"My little one, *I* will teach you."

"Oh, Father, I commit into Your hands my love for my husband. I commit into Your hands our whole marriage, our relationship, our communication, our time together, etc.

Father, I will not burden myself with something that I cannot touch, for only *You* can touch the heart. Father, it is a joy to leave this in *Your* hands."

"That is where it belongs, little one; that is where it belongs."

2 Timothy 1:12 (NKJV) For this reason I also suffer these things; nevertheless I am not ashamed, for I know whom I have believed and am persuaded that He is able to keep what I have committed to Him until that Day.

Proverbs 27:5
1 Corinthians 13:4-7

February 4

(Journal 3-3-1988)
　　"Thank You, Father, for letting me sit at Your feet and look into Your eyes. In those eyes I see running streams, mountains and waterfalls—everything that is beautiful."

Psalm 27:4 (NIV) One thing I ask of the LORD, this is what I seek: that I may dwell in the house of the LORD all the days of my life, to gaze upon the beauty of the LORD and to seek him in his temple.

Luke 10:39

February 5

(Journal 3-5-1988)
　　"Cleanse my heart, oh Lord. I want to be like You. My heart is grieved today because of *me*. Oh, Father, let my heart

be honoring to You. Let the gentleness of Jesus fill me. Thank You, Father."

"Little one, go in peace, for your Father has heard your heart and is here to heal. Lay awhile before My feet. Close your eyes and let My healing wash over you. Find peace as I gently bathe you in My love."

Psalm 51:1-2 (NKJV) Have mercy upon me, O God, according to Your lovingkindness; according to the multitude of Your tender mercies, blot out my transgressions. Wash me thoroughly from my iniquity, and cleanse me from my sin.

1 John 1:9
James 5:16
1 Peter 2:21-24

February 6

(Journal 4-10-1988)
"I see my weakness more and more...so frail. But in that weakness I see Your great and awesome power. I am humbled before You today to the point where I have to say, 'The only good thing that comes forth from me is because of Jesus.'"

"My little one, I will strengthen you and I will encourage you. My grace you shall not understand now, but you will, for I would desire to use you even in your weakness. Your faith is being built up; that faith which shall sustain you during trying times."

"Father, I loved worshipping You tonight at church. Thank You for putting that joy within my heart."

2 Corinthians 12:10 (NIV) That is why, for Christ's sake, I delight in weaknesses, in insults, in hardships, in persecutions, in difficulties. For when I am weak, then I am strong.

James 1:2-4
Colossians 2:6-7

————◆◆◆————

February 7

(Journal 7-26-1988)
     "Welcome, little one, rest in Me and do not consider your time with Me an intense struggle; not until I show you what is worth struggling over. Find peace. Drink it in and delight over the joys I have set before you. Give Me your hand and let Me lead you to what *I* consider important. Do not try to create your own tasks.
     My child, allow Me to speak to you throughout the day. Be attentive to My voice."

Psalm 90:17 (NIV) May the favor of the Lord our God rest upon us; establish the work of our hands for us—yes, establish the work of our hands.

Isaiah 26:12
John 10:27

————◆◆◆————

February 8

(Journal 8-18-1988)
     "Take the time to listen to Me, for I would tell you wonderful things and give you many comforts.

Know now, My children, that I love you; that My eyes are upon you and I will not leave you comfortless.

Though you do not yet know what direction I would have you take, tune your ear to listen. For soon, very soon, will I give word and then it will be time to act. Draw near to Me now. Find strength and joy in Me. Rest your weary body upon One who is strong; for strength and joy belong to Me. How freely would I give to the simplest one who would come and ask. It does not take a great heart to receive from God, but only an open heart, only a trusting heart.

Your needs soon will be many. Do you trust that I will meet these needs? Do you believe that your Father loves you? This is the real question. For in this belief comes the knowledge that all will be well; that the soul as well as the body will be fed. You are in need of comfort; it is your Father's joy to be a Comforter. Trust Me. You've trusted Me before, trust Me now."

As I was thinking of reading further in Exodus, I heard, **"It is fitting that you should read what you are reading now. Learn from it, My child, and apply it to your heart. I would that My children should learn from the mistakes of others and not make the same mistakes themselves."**

"I would wrap you in love as one wraps a little child in a blanket."

Jeremiah 33:3 (NKJV) "Call to Me, and I will answer you, and show you great and mighty things, which you do not know."

John 14:26 (KJV) "But the Comforter, which is the Holy Ghost, whom the Father will send in my name, he shall teach you all things, and bring all things to your remembrance, whatsoever I have said unto you."

Isaiah 51:12

Romans 15:4

February 9

(Journal 8-19-1988)
   "**My child, life shall change for you in many ways. In that change there is One who is stable, so cling to Me. Ah, My child, trust not in what the day will hold, but in the One who holds the day.**"

Malachi 3:6a (NIV) "I the LORD do not change."
Psalm 63:8
2 Samuel 22:47

February 10

(Journal 8-21-1988)
   "Speak to my heart, Lord. Teach me as I read Your word. Instruct me. Lead me in right paths. Thank you."

   "**It is My delight to instruct you, child. It is My joy to lead you in right paths. Rejoice that your Father finds your heart fit to lead; pliable in My hands.**"

Psalm 32:8 (NIV) I will instruct you and teach you in the way you should go; I will counsel you and watch over you.

Psalm 25:12
Proverbs 3:1-6

February 11

(Journal 8-26-1988)
      Yesterday, the Lord spoke the following:

      "My little one, I would desire to share something with you. The time is coming soon when I shall lead you forth. Very soon the cry shall ring out, 'The time has come.'
      My little one, I have given you gifts to disperse to those in need. Give as I would desire you to give. Do not let sentiments keep you from giving. Take only, with you, two boxes each and what you can hold in your suitcases. My little one, are you afraid to give away what you have? This would be My requirement of you."

      At first it was a hard thought. My biggest concern was for the people who had given us gifts. I didn't want them to ever feel bad.
      Last night John and I began going through boxes and separating what we would take from what we would give away. It wasn't easy. It was hard when John, after sharing a part of his life with me, dumped all of his music awards for singing, trombone, etc. in the wastebasket.
      The Lord has blessed John with a beautiful voice, but one no longer to be used in competition.

Luke 18:28 (NIV) Peter said to him, "We have left all we had to follow you!"

Luke 14:33
1 Timothy 6:6-8

February 12

(Journal 5-29-1989)
"I love You, Father. I love spending time in Your presence—listening, sharing."

"I love you too, My child. May your heart grow more and more warm toward Me as I share with you *My* heart toward *you*. Let dialogue with Me be sweet to your soul. Let it cause your heart to sing. Let it free you to think upon the graces of your Father toward all His creation. Let it cause you to stand amazed as you witness the ultimate truths I would share with you. Let it delight your heart and feed you with sweet wonders.
I love you, My child."

Psalm 119:27 (NIV) Let me understand the teaching of your precepts; then I will meditate on your wonders.

1 Chronicles 16:9-10

February 13

(Journal 5-29-1989)
I read the following, in a book called, *A Closer Walk*, by Catherine Marshall:

> *"Lord, I need your help in so many areas. How can I better hear your voice?"*

"You need to begin listening in the absolute quiet as you did during that summer long ago on Cape Cod. Remember how you lay on the day bed in the living room, pen and notebook in hand, in absolute stillness? I spoke to you then—and will again.

A morning Quiet Time should be that—not simply reading in this book or that. What I, your Lord, have to say to you is more important than the best wisdom of any author."

As I desired to have again, this Quiet Time that the Lord spoke to Catherine Marshall about, I became very aware of the vacuum cleaner that roared on the floor above me. Then I heard in my spirit, **"Do you feel that you need the peace and quiet *around* you in order to hear Me? No, child, the peace and quiet must come from within you."**

John 10:27 (NIV) "My sheep listen to my voice; I know them, and they follow me."

Isaiah 30:15

Marshall, Catherine. *A Closer Walk* (New Jersey: A Chosen Book 1986) 196

February 14

(Journal 7-20-1989)
"To spend time with You, Father, revives my soul."

Today is my birthday, and what a wonderful way to celebrate it. John and I are at Cascade State Park, and we are each spending time alone with our journals and the Lord on the rocky shore of Lake Superior.

I've positioned myself at a picnic table in order to read my Bible and write in my journal. Down below me, and off to the right, I can see and hear the waves caressing the rocky lake shore. What beauty! A short while ago I was sitting down by the waves, expressing my joy to the Lord about being here—spending this time with Him.

> Ah, sweet beauty,
> Man may seek your face,
> But you are found in fullness,
> In the arms of God's embrace.

That is where I have found beauty. If my spirit is not embracing the Spirit of God, beauty is like the shell of man without the breath.

Psalm 85:6 (NLT) Won't you revive us again, so your people can rejoice in you?

Psalm 23:3a (NKJV) He restores my soul...

Ecclesiastes 2:25 (NIV) ...for without him, who can eat or find enjoyment?

February 15

(Journal 12-7-1990)
In a dream, John and I were preparing for our wedding. A girl, with an excited voice said, "I have something you can wear with your wedding dress!" John, bending down, reached into a drawer and pulled out what she had to offer. It was white, sheer, lacy and tied around the waist. I looked at it critically and said, "I wouldn't wear that! It looks like an apron! I would look like a servant—or a slave!" John's gentle head was bent toward the item held in his hands. He slowly said, "Yes, maybe you would."
The dream ended there.
When I awoke, I thought of how the Lord desires for every bride to have a servant's heart toward her husband, and

how, in my dream, I had despised the role of a servant. I recommitted myself to serving John in love.

Mark 10:45 (NKJV) "For even the son of man did not come to be served, but to serve, and to give his life a ransom for many."

Galatians 5:13
1 Corinthians 11:9

February 16

(Journal 11-7-1992)
"I love you, My child.
I speak peace to your heart,
Calm to your spirit,
Love to your mind.
Remember these words."

John 14:27 (NKJV) "Peace I leave with you, My peace I give to you; not as the world gives do I give to you. Let not your heart be troubled, neither let it be afraid."

Philippians 4:7
2 Thessalonians 3:16

February 17

(Journal 11-10-1992)
"Little one, may your heart be a noble heart
and may your hands do noble things.
May the rain come to water your garden

and may the fruit of righteousness grow
up within you.
May your life be a life of ministering to others.
May your life be rich with the rewards of
work well done.
May your hand prosper where you place it
and may your face shine out the beauty of
your King.
May your spirit dwell by water
and may you find grace to help you all the
days of your life.
Go in peace, little one.
But in going, may you quickly return.
I love you, child."

2 Timothy 2:21 (NIV) If a man cleanses himself from the latter, he will be an instrument for noble purposes, made holy, useful to the Master and prepared to do any good work.

Psalm 1:1-3
Isaiah 58:11
Numbers 6:24-26

February 18

(Journal 11-12-1992)
"Oh child, you need to spend time with Me if you
are to fulfill your purpose on this earth. Let your
heart grasp for the truth. Let it delight to do the will
of God."

Psalm 40:8 (NIV) "I desire to do your will, O my God; your law is within my heart."

Ephesians 5:17 (NIV) Therefore do not be foolish, but understand what the Lord's will is.

Psalm 119:35
Psalm 1:2

February 19

(Journal 11-21-1992)

A quote from *The Believer's Secret of Obedience* by Andrew Murray:

> *Have we indeed given obedience that supreme place of authority over us that God means it to have, as the inspiration of every action and of every approach to Him? If we yield ourselves to the searching of God's Spirit, we may find that we never gave obedience the importance it deserves in our scheme of life, and that this is the cause of all our failure in prayer and in work. The deeper blessings of God's grace and the full enjoyment of God's love and nearness have been beyond our reach, simply because obedience was never made what God would have it to be—the starting point and the goal of our Christian life.*

Romans 1:5 (NIV) Through him and for his name's sake, we received grace and apostleship to call people from among all the Gentiles to the obedience that comes from faith.

1 John 2:5
1 John 5:3
2 Thessalonians 1:8

Murry, Andrew. *The Believer's Secret of Obedience* (Minneapolis: Bethany House, 1982), 21

February 20

(Journal 8-26-1993)

People go where people are because they feel that in the crowds they will find fulfillment; that somehow in the crowds they will find that which they are seeking, when they do not really even know what they are seeking. They do not know that the answer to their search is not found in the crowds, but in the lonely place of prayer. In this place, and this place only, is true fulfillment found.

I too have felt the restlessness. I too have sought the crowds, thinking *there* I would find a solution to the restless feeling. But it was only a temporary solution. When the fun was over, the emptiness returned.

I have found that the restlessness comes when we are neglecting our time alone with Jesus. If something feels missing in life, or wrong, or life feels unfulfilling, it is probably because we are running on empty. How wonderful it is when we remedy the problem, and life once again feels exciting, purposeful, beautiful and hopeful.

"Jesus, You alone hold the answer and remedy for our restlessness on earth."

Luke 5:16 (NIV) But Jesus *often* withdrew to lonely places and prayed.

Psalm 4:7 (NLT) You have given me greater joy than those who have abundant harvests of grain and new wine.

Psalm 16:11

February 21

(Journal 5-11-1997)
    In a vision, I saw a white marble pillar standing alone amidst chaotic destruction. There was fire, and bombing by aircraft still going on. The pillar was me. The rest was all that attacks or affects me emotionally, spiritually and physically.

    "If you would be encouraged, listen to this; My heart is open to you. The trials I send you are for your own good. I do not wish evil upon you. Stand firm. Stand fast. Joy in all I bring you. Delight to do My will."

James 1:2-4 (NIV) Consider it pure joy, my brothers, whenever you face trials of many kinds, because you know that the testing of your faith develops perseverance. Perseverance must finish its work so that you may be mature and complete, not lacking anything.

Ephesians 6:10-17
Psalm 75:3

February 22

(Journal 7-23-1997)
    I told John, how earlier in the day, I had an interesting, encouraging and momentarily sorrowful picture in my mind. I saw myself, as though looking from above. All around me, extending out like spokes on a wheel, were the people I knew—friends, family, acquaintances—the people I influence or have the potential to influence. Then I saw not only me, but everyone else, with their own circle around them. I wondered, "If everyone were to look at the spiritual health of a circle, what would it say about the prayer life of the person in the

middle? Would someone be able to look at the people standing around the person in the middle and see the fruit from a praying center or would one see sorrowful things as though looking at broken fences, dilapidated barns, souls ravaged by the enemy."

I wanted to pray more for those around me. I wondered, "What if the pictures of these people's lives were a picture of my prayer or lack of prayer for them." Obviously, many factors come into play, including their own bent toward sin. But, could I have influenced that 'bent' had I prayed more?

Ephesians 6:18 (NIV) And pray in the Spirit on all occasions with all kinds of prayers and requests. With this in mind, be alert and always keep on praying for all the saints.

Colossians 4:2
Colossians 1:9-12

February 23

(Journal 10-15-1997)
"Oh, My child, let your heart be the heart of a ready writer. Let My Spirit speak to you to encourage others. Don't stop writing because you feel you have no time. The time will come. I will open the way before you. I will give you the words to write. Look to Me.

Understand that My heart toward you is loving. Kindness flows from Me to My children. Rejoice, little one. Let your heart be glad that your Father loves you.

Speak comfort and encouragement to others. Delight the ears of those who listen to you. Leave off harshness, leave off anger. Let your heart be gentle toward the little ones in your charge.

Encouragement will flow from your pen as you make Me your source of inspiration. You have much

to discover. Do not think you have even begun to plumb the depths of all there is to discover about Me. Take delight in daily discoveries."

Psalm 45:1 (NKJV) My heart is overflowing with a good theme; I recite my composition concerning the King; my tongue is the pen of a ready writer.

1 Thessalonians 4:18 (NIV) Therefore encourage one another with these words.

1 Thessalonians 5:11

February 24

(Journal 4/1998)

"My little one, trust that all is well. Lean not unto your own understanding. Present your case before Me. Trust Me to see to your needs. Have I failed you yet? You may think that I have, but you are judging only by earthly appearances. You are not looking to the eternal perspective. Don't wallow in self-pity. I have come to redeem you from the pit; the pit of despondency, the pit of despair, the pit of aggression and depression, of self-hate and self-love to the extreme. My heart toward you is soft. My desire is not to crush you, but to lift you up on eagles' wings; to lift you to new heights of joy, love, peace, patience, goodness, self-control, humility, kindness and justice. Learn to trust Me again, child. Learn to lay all at My feet. Learn that I am trustworthy."

Titus 2:11-14 (NIV) For the grace of God that brings salvation has appeared to all men. It teaches us to say "No" to ungodliness and worldly passions, and to live self-controlled, upright and godly lives in this present age, while we wait for the blessed hope—the glorious appearing of our great God and Savior, Jesus Christ, who gave himself for us to redeem us from all wickedness and to purify for himself a people that are his very own, eager to do what is good.

Isaiah 40:31
Galatians 5:16-26
Proverbs 3:5

February 25

(Journal 5-10-1999)
"My little one, stretch out your hand to Me, for I would give you a little help. Pour out your heart to Me. Know that I am gentle with your faults. My desire is not to crush you, but to lift you up. Pay no attention to the enemy of your soul who would accuse you to yourself and cause you much grief. Listen instead to the voice of your Father who would speak encouragement to your soul. My gift to you is to shed blessing where now you sense guilt."

2 Thessalonians 2:16 (NIV) May our Lord Jesus Christ himself and God our Father, who loved us and by his grace gave us eternal encouragement and good hope, encourage your hearts and strengthen you...

1 Peter 5:6-8
Psalm 63:7-8

February 26

(Journal 5-18-1999)
     Something interesting...I wept and prayed and felt mercy for Charles Manson, the convicted killer, in prison for life. At the library I saw a 'new release' book with his name as the title. I picked it up and read only the back cover, because the library was closing in a few minutes. Tears and emotion for this man came—words flowed in prayer. I believed that I was feeling the Lord's heart. I prayed for his salvation. I prayed for mercy.
     Looking back, I remember the same tears, emotions, and desire for mercy and prayer for the drug lord, Noriega. I read some time later that he had become a Christian in prison.
     I wept and prayed also for Dahmer, the murderer and cannibal of young boys. Later, I learned that before he was murdered in prison, he had given his life to the Lord.
     I believe the Lord wants to save Charles Manson.

Nehemiah 9:17b (NLT) ...But you are a God of forgiveness, gracious and merciful, slow to become angry, and rich in unfailing love...

Luke 6:35b-36 (NIV) "...because he is kind to the ungrateful and wicked. Be merciful just as your Father is merciful."

Matthew 5:43-45
Ephesians 2:1-9

February 27

(Journal 6-17-1999)
     In my desire to cultivate the habit of prayer again, I came up with an idea—or perhaps it wasn't mine at all, but the Lord's. The idea is this: I will give myself one hour to pray each day. I bought a digital timer for this purpose. In the morning, I

set the timer for one hour, praying as long as I can and pausing the timer when I have to. I start the timer again each time I sit down at my desk to pray.

It is 1:35. I have spent a total of 15 minutes praying, out of the hour I've given myself to pray, praying in three different intervals. Even though I've prayed so little, I feel like I've been praying so long.

"Oh, Jesus, how little time I've given You through the years. But how I love this time with You now."

The timer is helping me to stay focused on prayer. I have a goal—to use up the time that the timer is giving me to pray. At first I thought this would cause my prayer to feel mechanical, but it doesn't. The timer is like the wardrobe Lucy used to enter the land of Narnia. Once inside His presence, the timer is irrelevant, only becoming important again as I exit the prayer closet to perform my duties.

The timer, for me, is a lovely gift of sixty wonderful minutes to spend with the Lord. It's actually a lot like a gift certificate which I have to spend by the end of the day or lose.

"My little one, you will see your life change before your eyes as you spend time with Me. You will see your life change with your husband and you will see your life change with your children."

"It's hard to believe that in less than 15 minutes with You, my heart can know such joy. Three or four worship songs have come to mind. Father, would You forgive me for my prayerlessness through the years?"

Spending time with God is the key to walking in the Spirit.

Colossians 4:2 (NIV) Devote yourselves to prayer, being watchful and thankful.

Romans 12:12
Psalm 109:4

February 28

(Journal 7-8-1999)
    Tonight my heart hears a distant call—a sweet echo remembered. It is this that has stirred my soul: "At midnight I rise to give you thanks for your righteous laws." *Psalm 119:62 (NIV)*
    I remember the yearning of a younger heart, to rise in the night and find sweet communion with Jesus; even praying that the Lord would wake me. Now, when children often wake us at odd hours, my heart does not cry for the Lord, but for sleep.

Psalm 63:6 (NIV) On my bed I remember you; I think of you through the watches of the night.

Isaiah 26:9a (NIV) My soul yearns for you in the night; in the morning my spirit longs for you.

Psalm 42:8
Luke 6:12

February 29

(Journal 7-19-1999)
    "Oh Lord, who wouldn't want to spend time with You, when I see my life changing before my eyes as You said it would. I didn't expect to see changes this soon. You are changing my heart. I love You so much. And what would life be like with You if I were spending even *more* time in Your presence?"

2 Corinthians 3:17-18 (NIV) Now the Lord is the Spirit, and where the Spirit of the Lord is, there is freedom. And we, who with unveiled faces all reflect the Lord's glory, are being transformed into his likeness with ever-increasing glory, which comes from the Lord, who is the Spirit.

Ezekiel 36:26

Mirrored Image
(Based on a true incident in college - 1980)

As I sat thinking, staring into space,
And contemplating much with time I had,
Accusing thoughts took form, and then a face,
Myself reflected, mirroring all the bad.
In mind, my fingers touched the hardened glass,
And helplessly I cried to no one there,
"I cannot change myself, I cannot pass
Through this separating wall of my despair!"
Then as I looked, my image faded out,
A face, a form, began to take its place.
I recognized my Lord without a doubt;
He spoke and I was showered by His grace,
    "My child, look instead at Me,
    I'm on both sides to set you free."

– Laura Kringle
(12/1989)

Gift of Beauty
(A true story)

As I wandered down the wooded path,
Following slowly behind the rest,
I stopped to freeze the gaze,
On which my eyes were blessed.

I knelt before the little form,
Of creation from God's hand—
A flower rich in beauty,
To grace a sojourner's land.

I looked to heaven and thanked the Lord
For the beauty of His touch.
Though only one little flower,
The sight had meant so much.

And as my eyes were lifted up,
His voice came in my heart,
"I made it for you," He said.
These words caused tears to start.

Years went by, and then one day,
As I pondered this event,
I realized He made it for everyone,
That is what He must have meant.

But just as this did cross my mind,
His words in my thoughts partook,
"I made it for you," He repeated...
"You're the only one who stopped to look."

– Laura Kringle
(8-16-85)

March 1

(Journal 8/ 1999)
    I asked the Lord tonight, "Why is it that I seem to stray so far from all the good things in Your word?" His answer came, **"By reading *Daily Bread*, you are only snacking."** I laughed, but recognized the truth of this. I need to go back to reading through the Bible, from cover to cover, *also.*

Psalm 119:10-11 (NIV) I seek you with all my heart; do not let me stray from your commands. I have hidden your word in my heart that I might not sin against you.

Psalm 119:105
Deuteronomy 17:18-20

March 2

(Journal 1-7-2000)
    Today, I chose to be a customer service person for God. I am here under His employment. I want to treat my family and others with kindness and meet their needs as though I were working in the customer service department for the Lord. I've often thought of how I would like to treat people if I were the customer service person behind the counter in a store—especially when treated rudely. Well, I have my opportunity, each and every day of my life, to treat people in a caring way.

Ephesians 4:31-32 (NKJV) Let all bitterness, wrath, anger, clamor, and evil speaking be put away from you, with all malice. And be kind to one another, tenderhearted, forgiving one another, even as God in Christ forgave you.

Matthew 7:12
Colossians 3:23-24

March 3

(Journal 1-19-2000)

People of Yesterday

People of yesterday,
Friends that I've known,
Semi-close relatives,
I've left to their own;
Those I have written to,
Perhaps once a year,
Now fill my heart,
For I wish to draw near.
I wish to revive,
Loving thoughts from the past,
And create from old memories
A love that will last.
It's the letters they've written,
A note or a card,
As I sift through my pile,
To save or discard,
That have caused me to love them,
Again, all anew,
And made me consider,
What it is I can do.
I've written to some,
Plan to phone yet another.
I've determined my dad,
And my own precious mother,
Will hear from me more,
In this year that's ahead.
I'll send them more letters,
Or visit instead.
People of yesterday,
Friends that I've known,

Harvesting love,
From words they have sown.
– Laura Kringle

Galatians 6:9 (NIV) Let us not become weary in doing good, for at the proper time we will reap a harvest if we do not give up. Therefore, as we have opportunity, let us do good to all people, especially to those who belong to the family of believers.

1 Peter 1:22
Hebrews 10:24

--------••▰▰◍◍▰▰••--------

March 4

(Journal 1-29-2000)
    I asked the lord this morning if He had a message for me. He said,
"Stand fast, little one, stand fast, and you will receive the praises of heaven."
    I asked Him, "How do I stand fast?"
    "By anchoring yourself to My words, as you are doing."
    (I had just been memorizing the book of Ephesians & Psalm 91.)

2 Thessalonians 2:15 (NIV) So then, brothers, stand firm and hold to the teachings we passed on to you, whether by word of mouth or by letter.

Matthew 7:24-27
Ephesians 6:10-17
1 Corinthians 15:1-2

March 5

(Journal 1-31-2000)

The Lord is indeed helping me to grow up. He is teaching me to finally shake off school-girl feelings at church and around friends and family, as well as with strangers—the feelings that cause us to wonder or even care if people like us, and the worry that we aren't saying or doing the 'right' things. I have ceased wondering why, or even caring, that people seem warm on one occasion and cool the next. *I* can choose to care about them regardless of their affections, or lack of them, toward me.

My desire is to be a warm, giving, unselfish person. I want to minister to those around me with the love and admonition of the Lord.

Colossians 3:16 (NIV) Let the word of Christ dwell in you richly as you teach and admonish one another with all wisdom...

Proverbs 29:25 (NIV) Fear of man will prove to be a snare, but whoever trusts in the LORD is kept safe.

Colossians 3:12-15

March 6

(Journal 2-4-2000)

This morning when I awoke, the Lord was speaking to me, **"It's time to slow down."** The impression of what He meant came to me, also. It's time to slow down my pace, my body movements—my actions. I had never considered that slowing down my pace and body movements could actually help calm anxious feelings and help me breath deeper. But this seems to be the present result.

I believe it will also be easier to hear from the Lord. It seems, perhaps, that He does not speak through flurry, or we do not hear Him.

I've been praying about my health; I think this is my first lesson.

Isaiah 50:4b (NIV) He wakens me morning by morning, wakens my ear to listen like one being taught.

Proverbs 19:20 (NIV) Listen to advice and accept instruction, and in the end you will be wise.

Proverbs 14:30 (NLT) A peaceful heart leads to a healthy body...

Psalm 143:8

———————

March 7

(Journal 2-23-2000)
I read something very valuable today in <u>The Christian Mother</u> by Jacky Hertz. It was this:

> *One of our teenage sons showed me how much our offspring rely on what they see. He had gone off to college and came back filled with fervor for the reading of the Holy Bible. He stopped in midsentence to look squarely at me. "Mom, why don't you ever try reading it? Our Bible just sits there for show." He pointed to the big picture Bible on the bookcase. "I do read it," I answered. "I just didn't think I had to read it in front of everybody. My Bible's by my bed. The one on this stand is beautiful, but it's too heavy to hold." I*

felt my face flush in annoyance and in sudden painful realization. Because I'd valued the peace and quiet as I read scripture passages, I hadn't understood I was cheating our kids of their share of inspiration.

What an inspiration and revelation this reading was to me. I realized I shouldn't always be trying to find time *alone* to pray. I should be including the children in my prayer time—at least including any that dare to knock on my door or enter when I'm trying to pray. The children *need* to see me praying. They need to have that secure picture to take with them all of their little lives. Also, they need to spend time praying with me so they can learn better how to pray, and learn that prayer is a friendship with God.

As I was praying this afternoon, little Nathan walked into the room. I reached for him and said, "Nathan, can you pray with Mama? We can pray for Heather because she is sick." Nathan knelt with me at my arm chair. He bent his little head forward and was quiet while I prayed. After a while he nestled in my lap. We prayed for the girls, Nathan, John, myself, and then some of my friends. When Nathan grew restless and got up, I said, "Nathan, do you want to sing a song with me?" A hymn had entered my mind during the joy of praying. I looked up the song in my hymn book and sang it through twice.

When Sarah was younger, I made her my little prayer partner when she would find me praying. I had forgotten about this.

Proverbs 22:6 (NKJV) Train up a child in the way he should go, and when he is old he will not depart from it.

2 Timothy 3:15
Psalm 127:3-5

Hertz Jacky, *The Christian Mother* (New York, Hawthorn Books, 1976), 70

March 8

(Journal 8-20-2000)

"Little one, do unto others as you would have others do unto you. Let your words be few and kind, in consideration of others. Do not feel or act as though you are center stage. Delight in putting others there. But if someone desires to put you there, oblige them. Delight in honoring one another above yourselves."

Romans 12:10 (NLT) Love each other with genuine affection, and take delight in honoring each other.

Matthew 7:12
Proverbs 17:27

March 9

(Journal 11-15-2000)

A moment ago I said, "Thank You, Jesus, for this pleasant day." I heard, **"Shall I give you a pleasant day and not also an unpleasant day?"** I realized I needed to thank the Lord for unpleasant days as well, for they are gifts to help me develop character and love. If I give God credit for giving me a pleasant day, then is He not also responsible for my unpleasant days? Yes, I must thank Him for those as well.

Job 2:10b (NIV) "Shall we accept good from God, and not trouble?"

Ecclesiastes 7:14 (NIV) When times are good, be happy; but when times are bad, consider: God has made the one as well as the other.

Lamentations 3:38 (NIV) Is it not from the mouth of the Most High that both calamities and good things come?

Isaiah 45:7 (NIV) "I form the light and create darkness, I bring prosperity and create disaster; I, the LORD, do all these things."

March 10

(Journal 8-23-2001)
    If I were to talk with another woman right now on the subject of marriage, I would tell her: "Find a picture of your husband that you like; stare into his face and pray for the man you see. Pray until the tears come. Pray until your emotions are touched. Keep praying God's heart for your husband."

1 Timothy 2:1 (NKJV) "Therefore I exhort first of all that supplications, prayers, intercessions, and giving of thanks be made for all men."

Romans 13:8-10
Proverbs 31:12

March 11

(Journal 4-6-2002)
    When you pray, dig deeper, past the shallow film of polite prayer and reach into honest, present, heart-felt prayer.

Share your heart. Share what is 'true' right now. It might be something like, "I'm having trouble praying, Lord, but I want to be close to You..." or whatever else is true for you. When you touch on 'truth,' emotions become involved. Once your emotions are engaged, praying becomes easier.

Psalm 62:8 (NKJV) "Trust in Him at all times, you people; pour out your heart before Him; God is a refuge for us."

Psalm 51:6

March 12

(Journal 6-12-2002)

Foolish Pride

As he left today,
I felt a chill;
The atmosphere was frozen—
Still.

I spoke to God, "What now...
What now?
What will bring back peace?"

The fault was mine,
I take the blame,
And had I taken then
The same...
We'd still be friends.

I spoke to God,
And, "This," He said,
"This will bring back peace..."

"Call him up—

Apologize,
And you will see your peace
Arise."

"But Lord,
I have my pride, you know.
It wouldn't do to let it go..."

"Okay, I'll do it."

(I did.)

Oh the foolishness of pride.

– Laura Kringle

Matthew 5:23-24 (NKJV) "Therefore, if you bring your gift to the altar, and there remember that your brother has something against you, leave your gift there before the altar, and go your way. First be reconciled to your brother..."

Hebrews 12:14
Proverbs 13:10

March 13

(Journal 6-12-2002)

John called himself, "The disciple whom Jesus loved" (John 21:20). I believe it was because he loved Jesus so much, and therefore had the confidence that Jesus loved him.

I used to think everyone at the table, during the last supper, heard Jesus say, "It is the one to whom I will give this piece of bread when I have dipped it in the dish" (John 13:26). I realize now, that even though Peter asked John to ask Jesus who it was that would betray him, only John, who leaned *close* to Jesus, heard his answer.

I believe those who are *close* to Jesus—who choose to *remain* close to him, are given 'insider' information that not everyone else hears or knows.

It wasn't until later, perhaps after the crucifixion, that John probably revealed to the other disciples what Jesus had told him, when Jesus gave the bread to Judas.

Oh, the mysteries of the Lord, revealed, when we spend time with Him.

Jeremiah 33:3 (NLT) "Ask me and I will tell you remarkable secrets you do not know about things to come."

John 13:25
John 21:20
John 14:21
Psalm 25:14

March 14

(Journal 8-13-2002)

I feel like I'm in love. There is someone who I've been spending time with. I love talking with him so much. He is such a good listener. When I'm with him I feel alive—energized. I've been sneaking away to be with him. We have found a quiet little out-of-the-way place to meet. He is so kind; I can share anything with him. He cares about every struggle and problem I have. The love I feel right now is amazing! The energy is pulsating through my limbs. I like the euphoric feeling I get just spending time with him, or thinking of spending time with him. Someday I'm going to be his bride. He doesn't seem to think he should take me away from my family just yet. That just shows one of the ways he is so considerate.

I wish every woman could know the excitement of a love like this.

John knows him, but I don't think he has any idea that I've been meeting with him in this quiet little out-of-the-way place. The funny thing is, when I'm spending time with him I find myself loving John more too! I even love my friends and family more. Like the old expression, "I'm walking on clouds"–I just want to pass this love on to everyone I meet.

I have to write his name in my journal. I'm not afraid for someone to see it.

His name is JESUS. I'm even going to divulge the secret place where we've been meeting—my bedroom closet. I've never met him there before; what a joy. I can talk with him out loud there, cry if I want, and no one hears but him. I have a little pad for my knees, a box to kneel over and a box of Kleenex at my side. I'm all set for a deeper relationship!

In the closet:

I can pray out loud.

I can sing.

I can lift my hands in praise.

No one else but the Lord is there to see me. No one can come upon me unaware. There is nothing to hinder my expression of praise to the Lord.

In my little cell of confinement there is great freedom. My spirit soars.

Psalm 45
Hosea 2:19-20

March 15

(Journal 8-19-2002)

The birds are so sweet. I used to wonder why they were sometimes such messy eaters. I would see them flipping their little beaks and scattering seeds out of the feeder on our deck. A few minutes ago, I watched three birds sitting in the feeder tray. Two of them were taking turns flipping seed out. Each bird would eat for a couple seconds, and then make two or three flipping motions as seed was flung from the feeder to the ground below. I followed my suspicions and ran downstairs to look out the window at the ground under the feeder. Sure enough, a half dozen or so birds were eating the seed that was being flung to them.

Yesterday, one of the girls noticed many birds on the ground when they looked out the same window. I knew they were eating the seed that fell, but I never guessed the birds were tossing seed down on purpose.

(Journal 12-21-2002)
Just as I am delighted to see our kids sharing their Sunday School snacks and Wednesday church treats with each other, I imagine the Lord is delighted when He sees us sharing with others from the blessings He has given us.

Hebrews 13:16 (NKJV) But do not forget to do good and to share, for with such sacrifices God is well pleased.

Romans 12:13

March 16

(Journal 8-29-2002)
I feel the Lord has given me a very precious gift. Tonight, at the Walmart store, I saw a book that took my breath away, and not just because of the beautiful antique-gold cover; it was, *Come Away My Beloved* by Francis J. Roberts. I felt the Lord was telling me in my spirit to get it—that it was a gift from Him.

As I held the book close to my heart and wandered through the store, I delightedly said to the Lord, "You are my Beloved." Without being consciously aware of my action, I held the book away from me and turned it over to reveal the back cover. My eyes landed on the words, "You are God's beloved." Delight burned within me again as I considered this His beautiful response to me.

Colossians 3:12 (NIV) Therefore, as God's chosen people, holy and dearly loved...

Romans 9:25-26 (NKJV) As He says also in Hosea: "I will call them My people, who were not My people, and her beloved, who was not beloved. And it shall come to pass in the place where it was said to them, 'You are not My people,' there shall they be called the sons of the living God."

Ephesians 5:1
2 Thessalonians 2:13

—————

March 17

(Journal 9-14-2002)
   "Thank You for teaching me that when I feel I cannot pray, I can always praise. I can *always* thank You for things. I could go on forever thanking You."

   Some might say, "I can't think of anything, right now, to thank God for." I would say, "Begin like this: 'Thank You, Father, for this chair I am sitting on (or this carpet I'm kneeling on). Thank You for this house this chair is in...' From there you can never run out of things for which to thank God."

Psalm 100:4 (NKJV) Enter into His gates with thanksgiving, and into His courts with praise. Be thankful to Him and bless His name.

Psalm 75:1
Psalm 50:14

March 18

(Journal 12-5-2002)
We are like millionaires who have the ability to affect hundreds of thousands of lives, and more. Every day we have minutes at our disposal to think idle thoughts or to invest in the lives of others, by praying for them. How foolish of me to waste time thinking of myself or some other trivial thing, when I could be praying and changing the world.

Do we believe in the God who tells us, "Ask and you shall receive?" Do we really believe in prayer? How foolish of us, then, to waste our lives on silly concerns.

I might not always have money to give away to help someone, but I can pray for people's spiritual or emotional well-being.

The enemy would have us concentrate upon ourselves, our pains and pleasures, in order to keep us from affecting the world for good. Reading books can keep us from prayer. Writing can keep us from prayer. Oh, the exciting world we leave untouched in exchange for a few moments to ourselves. Sometimes we touch only our own lives when we could be touching many lives.

"Father, forgive us for our selfishness."

Ephesians 6:18 (NIV) And pray in the Spirit on all occasions with all kinds of prayers and requests. With this in mind, be alert and always keep on praying for all the saints.

Philippians 2:4
2 Corinthians 1:11

March 19

(Journal 3-19-2003)
"I feel bathed in Your love."

"Oh little one, I would refresh you every day, as with a shower, if you would but come to Me."

Acts 3:19 (NIV) "Repent, then, and turn to God, so that your sins may be wiped out, that times of refreshing may come from the Lord..."

Matthew 11:28
2 Corinthians 4:16

March 20

(Journal 5-13-2003)
This is the first day I have been able to see interruption during my quiet time as 'from the Lord.' He has caused me to realize that interruptions are from Him. Oh, the sweet moments I have missed because of turning the children away during my quiet times.

Mary came in and asked if she could read to me. I put my arm around her as she read a page of her book to me. What a precious time. Then I told her I was taking a quiet time and she left, shutting the door behind her.

Shortly after that, Heather came in to record, on the book list at the back of our bedroom door, two books she had read. I called her over for a hug first, and talked with her about the books she had read.

I love this. How seldom I seem to have time alone with each child. I didn't realize all the opportunities I was missing. "Father, forgive me."

Nathan came in to ask how to spell 'kitchen.' I hugged him as he wrote.

Heather came over for another hug before she left. Heather then asked me what I was doing. I told her I was taking a quiet time—that I was reading in Romans.

I know the Lord is able to give me uninterrupted time as well, so if the interruptions come, let them come. I will take advantage of the opportunity to love my children.

As I bent my head to pray just now, I seemed to sense Him saying, **"You *have* spent time with Me."**

I look expectantly for the next interruption. The Lord wants to love His children through me.

Mark 9:35-37 (NIV) Sitting down, Jesus called the Twelve and said, "If anyone wants to be first, he must be the very last, and the servant of all." He took a little child and had him stand among them. Taking him in his arms, he said to them, "Whoever welcomes one of these little children in my name welcomes me; and whoever welcomes me does not welcome me but the one who sent me."

Mark 10:14-16
Matthew 25:40

March 21

(Journal 10-10-2003)
I had a wonderful autumn walk this morning before lunch. I was driven out doors by an anxiety in my spirit and a need to be alone. I started my walk in heaviness and ended it in joy. It is so good to walk and talk with the Lord.

The sun was shining and the wind was blowing, scattering the leaves before me. I walked around the pond, my

Sea of Galilee, and on toward the little woods. At one point, a breeze was flipping little gold leaves on the path ahead of me. The action gave the illusion of shimmering gold, sparkling on the sidewalk. The wind blew leaves off of the trees near the woods. With a delight that comes only from the Lord, I leapt from the ground to catch a falling leaf. The wind sent a shower of leaves upon me, but the only thing I caught was *laughter*.

Psalm 28:7 (NIV) The LORD is my strength and my shield; my heart trusts in him, and I am helped. My heart leaps for joy and I will give thanks to him in song.

Psalm 126:2-3
Luke 1:47

March 22

(Journal 11-6-2003)

It was a cold, blustery day today, yet the sunshine added to my delight when I sensed in my spirit the Lord saying, **"Come walk with Me."**

We hadn't walked far, when in the middle of my audible prayer, the Lord's inaudible words burst in, telling me to join the Toastmasters group. Then He added, **"If I call you to a task, I will equip you; and sometimes that equipping comes through regular means."**

I called Toastmasters International when I got home. The recording said they were a non-profit organization which helps people develop communication and leadership skills while building self-confidence.

That sounds exactly like what I need.

Hebrews 13:21 (NLT) May he equip you with all you need for doing his will. May he produce in you, through the power of Jesus Christ, every good thing that is pleasing to him. All glory to him forever and ever! Amen.

2 Timothy 3:17

March 23

(Journal 2/2004)

I was telling the Lord that I didn't have a very good memory—that I so easily forget important things. (There was a tinge of accusation in my attitude.)

In my spirit I heard, **"No one has a great memory, for the most part."** The Lord brought the image of Solomon to mind, and I thought of how the wisest man who ever lived forgot to not take many wives, to not go back to Egypt for horses, and to not worship other gods.

We all need to keep reviewing what is good and important every day. Like manna on the ground, our memories fade away. The word of God fades from our memory if we do not eat it (read it) every day.

Psalm 119:97 (NKJV) Oh, how I love your law! It is my meditation all the day.

Deuteronomy 17:16-20
1 Kings 10:26 - 11:4

March 24

(Journal 3-2-2004)

After all these years of frustration, on John's part, I finally realized I could make my stealing of the blankets at night, a prayer matter. Now, for the past two mornings, *I* am the one who has woken up short of blankets. Praise the Lord! I jokingly told John, "Now *you're* the one stealing the blankets."

Another thing I've lived with, but didn't think to pray about lately, is my complexion. A few days ago, I asked the Lord if He would clear up my complexion. Yesterday, while shopping, it entered my mind to check the ingredients on the facial cleanser I've been using. To my surprise, I saw the word 'sulfate.' I'm allergic to sulfur, and have noticed that make-up with sulfate in it will cause my face to break out. I bought a new cleanser. I think it may be the answer. This morning I noticed that the inflammation was diminished.

(Journal 11-7-2004)
My face has been pretty clear ever since. Praise the Lord!

When we see the Lord answering little personal prayers, it helps us trust Him with the prayers for which we will never see physical answers.

Philippians 4:6 (NKJV) Be anxious for nothing, but in everything by prayer and supplication, with thanksgiving, let your requests be made known to God;

Psalm 28:6-7
Psalm 123:1-2

March 25

(Journal 3/2004)
For five years I have put up with my curling-iron cord getting caught on the bathroom drawer and cabinet handles while I curled my hair. Finally, frustrated with the situation, I prayed, "Lord, is there a better way to do this?" In my heart I believed the Lord could help me find a better way. After praying, my hand moved almost instinctively, to open the top drawer and the bottom cabinet. My curling iron cord fell nicely

down the side of the open drawer and down the side of the open cabinet door. My cord entanglement problem was gone in seconds.

It's amazing what happens when we ask for the Lord's help, and more amazing still, when we don't.

As I thanked the Lord for helping me with the curling-iron problem, I heard: **"I am here, little one, to help you with every problem you have. No problem is too great for Me to solve."**

There are times I have asked in frustration, and with a complaining attitude, for the Lord's help. At those times, no answer seemed to come. I realize now, that my attitude was wrong. I was not asking with a listening heart, expecting to receive.

James 1:6-7 (NIV) But when he asks, he must believe and not doubt, because he who doubts is like a wave of the sea, blown and tossed by the wind. That man should not think he will receive anything from the Lord;...

Psalm 46:1
Psalm 30:10
Psalm 34:6

March 26

(Journal 3-22-2004)

"My little one, walk in My ways. Walk in My Spirit and you will not fulfill the lusts of the flesh.

Know that I love you, and that I am not quick to find offense. Know that you are sealed for the day of redemption, that your inheritance is in Me; that in Me lies all the treasures of wisdom and understanding. These I open up to you as you seek My counsel, as you seek understanding. Do not be short sighted, but 'come.' Do not come only when it is convenient. Do

not come only when it pleases you. Come because I have called you. Come because you are My child. Come because I love you."

Galatians 5:16 (NKJV) I say then: Walk in the Spirit, and you will not fulfill the lust of the flesh.

Ephesians 4:30
Colossians 2:2-3

———————————

March 27

(Journal 3-26-2004)
On my walk this afternoon, I came upon four boys fishing in a large pond. They looked to be around ten or eleven years old. Each had his own pole.

"Have you caught anything?" I asked. The shortest boy, who had wavy reddish-blond hair, turned toward me and said, "Yeah, seventeen Northern." He seemed sincere. "So they put fish in there," I commented, as the boys were leaving. As I followed behind them on the path, I heard snickering. The taller boy, on a skateboard, said mockingly, "Seventeen Northern!"

"So he wasn't telling the truth," I thought, as I stared at their backs. I prayed for them that they would learn to love truth.

As I walked around a larger connected pond, I came upon the boys fishing in a new spot. "Should I say something to the boy, Lord?" I asked. "Help me to know." I was about to pass them, when the boy who spoke with me earlier, turned his mirthful face toward me. I walked down a short path to the boys. There were only three of them now; the one on the skateboard had left. "I heard your friend laughing about you catching seventeen Northern." "We exaggerated," he said with a smile, "but we have caught *some* fish." I put my hand on his shoulder and said, "Learn to love truth. Jesus is truth." "Yeah," he said.

I left, after laughing with them over a rubber duck decoy one of the boys had dragged in.

I prayed for the boys as I walked around the pond. I prayed the red-haired boy would never forget my words.

Zechariah 8:19b (NKJV) ...Therefore, love truth and peace.
2 Thessalonians 2:10
John 18:37-38
John 14:6

March 28

(Journal 5-3-2004)

I had a wonderful experience in prayer this afternoon. While walking around the pond, I invited the Holy Spirit to come and lead me in prayer. Suddenly, into my mind came the vision of a dove swooping down to pick me up and carry me on its back over the ocean. It was an exhilarating sensation. I thought of the verse in Genesis that speaks of the Spirit of God hovering over the waters (Gen. 1:1-2).

From the air, I saw the continent of China, and the dove flew down into the country. I saw people in a prison, and was led to pray for the persecuted Christians in China, their families, the people they were influencing and the leaders. Then the dove lifted off from China, and I found we were approaching the mountains of Tibet. I prayed for the monks and the people of Tibet. I prayed for the darkness to be removed and for the Lord's light to come.

From Tibet, we went to the dark continent of Africa. I prayed for the Lord's Spirit to continue to sweep through the continent and bring light, brotherly love, unity and healing.

I then felt the dove leading me to pray for myself, and for my own family. We flew to my home town, and I saw the water tower I had lived near. I prayed for people there.

I love it when the Lord leads.

Ezekiel 11:24-25 (NIV) The Spirit lifted me up and brought me to the exiles in Babylonia in the vision given by the Spirit of God. Then the vision I had seen went up from me, and I told the exiles everything the LORD had shown me.

Matthew 3:16
Romans 8:14

March 29

(Journal 5-15-2004)
    I'm excited! I have just discovered God's cues to pray. A wet towel on the floor, flung there by a child, whom I have had to tell over and over again, "Don't throw your towel on the floor," is my cue to pray, "Father, please help (child's name) to have wisdom and to do what is right. Please help her to love righteousness..." Every object lying around the house that shouldn't be there, every unfinished job, every accident, is my cue to pray for the person involved. Instead of letting these things irritate me, I can let them be my driving force to pray for my children's characters, attitudes and futures.
    The things that have irritated me will become a source of joy, if I see them as my cues to pray.
    "Thank You, Father."

Proverbs 19:11 (NIV) A man's wisdom gives him patience; it is to his glory to overlook an offense.

Ephesians 4:1-2

March 30

(Journal 6-5-2004)
"A woman of grace and beauty has learned to hold her tongue."

I sensed the Lord telling me this as I walked around the pond. It was so good to hear Him speaking with me again—teaching me. The Holy Spirit had seemed pretty silent for weeks. I was pleasantly surprised by the Lord's communication with me, following my repentance in the area of gossip. The Lord confirmed in my thoughts that His silence was directly related to me speaking out against someone—actually more than *one* someone. He brought to my mind numerous people that I had defamed to my husband within the last few weeks.

I never thought I was one given to gossip. But in reading the book, *A Woman's High Calling*, by Elizabeth George, I was made aware of my involvement. Was it necessary for me to pass on updated information concerning a pastor caught in adultery? Why let such information ever cross my lips?

I find if I hold my tongue when tempted to speak, the words have to come out somewhere. If I stop them at my mouth, they turn course and are directed up to the Lord through prayer. This seems a better way for me to live. If I spout off at the mouth, my desire to pray for a situation or person is relieved, and I find it difficult, if not impossible, to regain the fervency that would have lifted my heart to the Lord.

Elizabeth George helped me to see that even passing on true information about someone can be gossip. It's even worse if I'm only passing on suspicions.

Just as we might feel hurt, protective or angry if we hear someone speaking out against one of our children, we must take into consideration the Lord's protectiveness toward His children, or those who might become His.

Proverbs 10:19 (NKJV) In the multitude of words sin is not lacking. But he who restrains his lips is wise.

1 Peter 3:10-11
Psalm 15:1-3
Matthew 12:36

<hr>

March 31

(Journal 6-27-2004)

If we attempt to keep our thoughts pure before God, we will more easily recognize the enemy when he comes, because His thoughts will be so contrary to our own.

On this relaxing Sunday afternoon, I sat in my bedroom with the door shut, reading the Bible in my cranberry colored arm chair. Suddenly, I started thinking about John not wanting, apparently, to spend time with me. I closed my Bible to dwell on these thoughts of self-pity. I immediately recognized the enemy. These were not *my* thoughts! I had been *enjoying* my time alone.

Shortly after I said, "No" to the enemy, John popped into the room, saying he had come to read with me.

What might have been the result of our afternoon if the first words out of my mouth had been an *accusation* when I saw John?

James 4:7b (NIV) Resist the devil, and he will flee from you.
John 10:10
Psalm 19:14

<hr>

Satan will plant a thought
and then accuse you for thinking it,
when it was not your thought
to begin with.

We get to know *about* Jesus
through His word.
We get to know Him *personally*
on our knees.

April 1

(Journal 8-16-2004)

A moment ago I was crying, feeling the Christian life was overwhelming, with too much to do—too much to remember. Into my misery came a gentle thought, **"Live in the moment. Is life overwhelming right now?"**

"What?" My voice was stilled and my tears held in suspension. I thought about my present situation. It was 9:15 in the evening. The kids were in bed, John was watching the Olympics and I was sitting in my cranberry armchair behind closed doors in a peaceful room. No, life was not overwhelming at the present. I was adding the past to the future. That's what made life seem overwhelming. If I live in my moment right now, it's actually very pleasant. I love time alone with the Lord—time to read my Bible.

"Thank You, Father, for the reminder to live in the moment."

Matthew 6:34 (NIV) "Therefore do not worry about tomorrow, for tomorrow will worry about itself. Each day has enough trouble of its own."

2 Thessalonians 3:16

April 2

(Journal 1-26-2005)

I asked the Lord today, during my confused, anxious state, how to live the Christian life. In my spirit I heard one word, **"Trust."** He filled me with warm memories of another time, when I would pray and ask the Lord for something concerning my life and then simply thank Him, believing He would do it.

Today, as I prayed, and thanked Him afterward, peace settled upon my spirit once more. He led me again to that place of rest. Confidence came. Some verses came to mind:

- "In repentance and rest is your salvation, in quietness and trust is your strength..." (*Isaiah 30:15b NIV*).
- The fruit of righteousness will be peace; the effect of righteousness will be quietness and confidence forever (*Isaiah 32:17 NIV*).

Philippians 4:6-7
Psalm 29:11

April 3

(Journal 3-16-2005)

"You have sought Me from the time you were young. You have desired to have a heart devoted to Me. Oh, My child, I would fill you full. Take and receive. Let your heart register 'full' instead of 'empty.' Spend time in My presence and you will never want for My presence. Those who lose My presence are really only losing time spent with Me. Take and eat. I would satisfy you with the richest of fare. You are lovely in My sight and I delight in delighting you. Take joy, little one, in My love for you. Take joy in the delights I give you. Rejoice that your Father loves you and finds you pliable in His hands. I delight to speak with you, to share with you from My treasure house of wisdom. Laid out before you is a table rich in fare, filled with choicest fruits and meat to satisfy your longing. You have yearned for Me. I am here. Lay hold, little one; lay hold of Me and do not let go. I would bring you often to this banquet if you would come to Me and delight yourself in Me. Yours, little one, is the treasure set before you; yours for the taking."

"Oh Father, my heart delights in You! I love You so much; I know it is with the love and emotion that *You* have given me right now. I long to live in Your presence, to delight myself always in You. Thank You for encouraging my heart tonight."

Psalm 63:5 (NIV) My soul will be satisfied as with the richest of foods; with singing lips my mouth will praise you.

Isaiah 55:1-3
Matthew 26:26

April 4

(Journal 7-26-2005)
      "My Little one, the words of My children are precious in My ears. Do not fear that I would silence you before Me. Bring your griefs, your fears, your joys, and lay them at My feet."

Psalm 55:22 (NIV) Cast your cares on the LORD and he will sustain you...

Lamentations 2:19
Psalm 62:8

April 5

(Journal 10-20-2005)
      Yesterday, I saw how our life is like a paddle wheel. All of the things we could or should do are on this wheel that is

constantly revolving. It's up to us, using wisdom from the Lord, to determine what things are priorities for us. We will never get done with all there is to do. Life is not like a ladder, where we will one day reach the top and suddenly have time for something.

People who say, "I don't have time for that," really mean, "It's not one of the things I choose to make a priority right now."

Seeing this illustration of the wheel, which I believe came from the Lord, helps me understand the importance of making a list to determine priorities in life. I'm never going to *find* the time for drawing or writing or finishing projects if I don't decide those things are priority. The wheel isn't going to stop. There will always be new and old things pulling at my attention, begging for my time.

What things will I choose from this wheel to make a priority?

Psalm 90:17 (NIV) May the favor of the Lord our God rest upon us; establish the work of our hands for us—yes, establish the work of our hands.

Proverbs 16:3
Proverbs 2:6

April 6

(Journal 2-6-2006)
<u>Morning:</u>
I am a servant in my Father's house. While I am getting ready for the day, every knock on my door is a pull of the bell cord, summoning my service. Who am I to complain or feel irritated when having to assist someone in need, even if the need is minor and one that, in my eyes, could wait. I must take each interruption as an opportunity to practice the patience of a servant. I want to hear, "Well done, good and faithful

servant." While I am going about my duties and someone interrupts me, I must see that interruption as the summons of the bell cord pulled by my Master.

Evening:
What I read in *God Calling* tonight goes along with what I wrote this morning. "Oh, Lord, help me to remember this lesson." The following is the devotion I read:

> *Extra work - October 10*
> *"...Take every duty and every interruption as of My appointment. You are My servant. Serve Me as simply, cheerfully and readily as you expect others to serve you. Do you blame the servant who avoids extra work, who complains about being called from one task to do one less liked? Do you feel you are ill-served by such a one? Then what of Me? Is not that how you so often serve Me? Think of this. Lay it to heart and view your day's work in this light."*

Matthew 25:21 (NIV) "His master replied, 'Well done, good and faithful servant! You have been faithful with a few things; I will put you in charge of many things. Come and share your master's happiness!'

John 12:26
Deuteronomy 28:47
Psalm 100:2a (NKJV) Serve the Lord with gladness...

———————

April 7

(Journal 5-4-2006)
"Lord, what is causing me to act so unchristian?"
"Lack of prayer."
"Can that be true?" (Wondering if it was the Lord I heard.)

"How much time have you spent on your knees today?"

My heart burst with emotion—I knew the truth. I rushed to my knees. These words came immediately:

"If you will give yourself to prayer and the study of My word, I will fill your life so full of My Spirit that you will not have room enough to receive it."

"Oh, Lord, I long for You. I long to walk and move and live in Your Holy Spirit—to be used mightily."

"Keep singing, little one, keep singing." (I used my hymnbook two times today. I wondered about it helping me to be able to pray.)

"If you remain in Me, little one, you have an exciting life opening up before you. Do not close the door with prayerlessness again. Do not let the enemy distract you from Me."

"Father, help me to see praying, singing and praising as the most important things I can do in a day."

1 Peter 4:7b (NIV) Therefore be clear minded and self-controlled so that you can pray.

Ephesian 5:18-19
John 15:1-8

———

April 8

(Journal 7-22-2006)

I sensed the Lord telling me tonight, **"Follow the path of peace. There is always a path of peace."** He also said, **"Seek peace and pursue it."**

If I run into inner turmoil, I have left the path of peace. I need to keep seeking out the path of peace.

Proverbs 3:17 (NIV) Her ways [wisdom] are pleasant ways, and all her paths are peace.

Luke 1:79 (NIV) "to shine on those living in darkness and in the shadow of death, to guide our feet into the path of peace."

Psalm 34:14

April 9

(Journal 8-16-2006)
"Learn to do things at the time it enters your mind to do it. I am trying to help you."

I need an 'ideal,' and *Fascinating Womanhood* provides that ideal. I was washing the dishes when the idea came to read *Fascinating Womanhood* and pray concerning our marriage. I considered reading it when the dishes were done, and that's when I heard, **"Learn to do things at the time it enters your mind to do it. I am trying to help you."**

I dried my hands and went to my room, all the while thinking of the times the Lord encouraged me to do things, but losing the opportunity, because I waited too long to do them.

As I read, I cried and prayed over the ways I had been controlling. I was reminded to trust the Lord to work in John, and to lead me through him.

"Thank you, Father. I love You."

Psalm 119:60 (NIV) I will hasten and not delay to obey your commands.

Psalm 146:5

Note: I use *Fascinating Womanhood* as an inspiration for prayer. I do not back everything said within its pages, though I find much of it very helpful and encouraging.

April 10

(Journal 9-3-2006)
    Allergies, through the years, have made me so miserable and irritable. Itchy throats, sore throats, as well as sneezing and other symptoms have provoked me to cry out to the Lord in desperation, "Lord, please heal me of my allergies! Take them away!"

    However, a new thought came last night, "How can I *use* my allergies and anchor them to something good?" I decided to praise the Lord every time I had a symptom. With every cough or sneeze, I would thank Him for someone or something. I would use the letters of the alphabet to think of the names of people to pray for, moving to the next letter each time I sneezed. I also remembered songs and verses that started with the letters. So, between sneezes, I would quote verses and sing songs, praying for everyone I could think of whose name started with the current letter.

    Suddenly my allergies became a joy. They were going to help me remember to praise the Lord, to be thankful, to pray for people, and to remember songs and verses! The Lord is good!

    Right now I'm on the letter 'B'. While using a lot of tissues, I've had an enjoyable time thinking of things and people to be thankful for.

    This could become a wonderful habit in my life.

1 Timothy 2:1 (NLT) I urge you, first of all, to pray for all people. Ask God to help them; intercede on their behalf, and give thanks for them.

Ephesians 6:18
Ephesians 5:20
Psalm 104:33

April 11

(Journal 9-4-2006)

(9:30 a.m.) Yesterday morning I went forward in church and asked the elders to pray for me concerning my allergies, which have seemed worse this year than ever. The idea from the Lord, to have the elders pray, came very soon after the idea of praying through the alphabet with every sneeze. Imagine me hesitating to go forward for prayer to have my allergies healed because I was so excited about thanking and praising the Lord with every allergic symptom! Still, I wanted to "fulfill all righteousness" (Matthew 3:15), and ask for prayer as scripture says to do (James 5:14).

You know what? This morning, I didn't wake up sneezing, using tissues or scratching my throat! I sneezed once today, so I'm on the letter 'M'. Last night I was on 'L'.

I had such an enjoyable time thanking and praising the Lord yesterday, and praying for people. I also enjoyed thinking of verses and songs. I felt like I spent the whole day in the presence of Jesus, and what a joy it was!

Yesterday I had cheese for supper. Always, when I have dairy the day before, I wake up sneezing and feeling miserably itchy. I always think, "Pizza isn't worth it!"

This morning I woke up with absolutely no symptoms, except a slight sore throat, which I've had for months.

It's 10:45 in the morning and I haven't sneezed yet! I even dusted the furniture and shook out my duster! A few times I felt the tingle of a sneeze coming on, but after a couple seconds the tingle stopped. My expectation of moving on to letter 'N' has been dashed time and again. Oh, disappointed, happy me.

It's 6:25 p.m. and I'm still on the letter 'M'! Numerous times today I thought I was going to sneeze. The tingling would come, but then just fade away. I'm going to try changing letters and praying for new people whenever I feel the tingling.

James 5:14 (NIV) Is any one of you sick? He should call the elders of the church to pray over him and anoint him with oil in the name of the Lord.

Matthew 3:15
Mark 16:18

———————————

April 12

(Journal 9-23-2006)

A while ago, we moved our silverware to a different drawer in the kitchen. It took weeks, almost a month, before we even began to look in the right drawer without first reaching for the wrong one. Realizing, this morning, how long it took to form a new habit with the silverware, I had renewed hope and joy at the thought that at least I'm moving in the right direction with my 'Things to Remember' list (changes I want to implement in my life). As I keep being aware of the things I want to change, eventually change will happen. There is no need to feel discouragement because things are taking longer than I would like.

For example, in trying to 'see interruption as from the Lord,' I've made many mistakes. I would usually think about what my reaction to interruption *should* have been, after the fact. But if I use the illustration of stopping a train, I at last began seeing the wheels slowing down and I can now say the wheels have started going in reverse. I'm now remembering *before* I have a negative reaction, to see interruption as from the Lord. I'm even anticipating interruption ahead of time and thinking of how I will respond. Praise the Lord, change is happening.

When I see how long it can take for me to change, it makes me want to be so much more patient with little children. Let's be patient, and tell them something every day for a month instead of impatiently saying, "How many times do I have to tell you?" The answer to that question is, "At least a month's worth!" We sometimes think it is awful if we have to say something twice!

Ephesians 4:2 (NIV) Be completely humble and gentle; be patient, bearing with one another in love.

Proverbs 14:29

April 13

(Journal 10/2006)
John and I prayed together concerning the large intense fire that is out of control in California, about thirty miles from Palm Springs. Homes are being destroyed, and a number of fire fighters have lost their lives. We prayed for the fire to be put out, for the fire fighters, and for the people losing their homes.

Alone in my bedroom, I asked the Lord, "What should we be praying?" I heard, **"Pray that they might escape the flames of hell."** This is God's perspective. How important are the flames destroying homes *compared* to the flames of hell destroying souls?

Matthew 10:28 (NIV) "Do not be afraid of those who kill the body but cannot kill the soul. Rather, be afraid of the One who can destroy both soul and body in hell."

Jude 1:23
1 Timothy 1:15
Acts 2:38
Luke 13:2-5

April 14

(Journal 11-14-2006)
About Jesus: Go find His face and hug Him before you start making requests of Him. Be like a child coming home from school who goes into the kitchen to find his mother and give her a hug, instead of rushing in the door, slamming down books and calling out, "Can I have something to eat? I'm starved!"

I had a sweet time with Jesus tonight because He led me to seek His face before I brought to Him my troubles. Words and songs of praise spilled from my lips, out of emotions I felt, while kneeling in His presence.

Psalm 27:8 (NIV) My heart says of you, "Seek his face!" Your face, LORD, I will seek.

Psalm 105:3-4
Isaiah 55:6

April 15

(Journal 11-14-2006)
With things troubling my mind, I knelt in prayer and told the Lord, "I feel so out of control." He gently asked, **"Are things out of *My* control?"** I thought for a second and then answered, "No, I guess they're not," as the realization of what He was getting at struck me. He spoke again, **"Then why are you so troubled?"** I realized then, I had no reason to be.

Daniel 4:34b-35 (NIV) His dominion is an eternal dominion; his kingdom endures from generation to generation. All the peoples of the earth are regarded as nothing. He does as he pleases with the powers of heaven and the peoples of the earth. No one can hold back his hand or say to him: "What have you done?"

Psalm 24:1
Ecclesiastes 7:14
Lamentations 3:37-39

April 16

(Journal 12-5-2006)

The Lord gave me a fun idea today. Rather than just tell the kids to clean up their rooms, I gave them the choice of a nickel or a sugar-free Ice-Breaker candy for each job I assigned. The jobs were things such as dusting a shelf and making it look nice again, cleaning up one small area of the room at a time, finding a new home for some new books, putting away their washed socks and underwear. The kids had fun cleaning up and so did I. The whole experience was zero frustration for all involved. I didn't even spend a whole dollar for such a pleasant time.

(The fun isn't over yet; Heather just came to me after their snack break to ask about doing more jobs.)

Proverbs 31:27 (NIV) She watches over the affairs of her household and does not eat the bread of idleness.

Titus 2:4-5

April 17

(Journal 12-21-2006)
    As I poured out my heart to the Lord, wondering how I could change, I heard in my spirit, **"Kindness is a choice, in each and every situation, not a permanent character change."**

    "Father, help me to choose kindness."

Titus 2:4-5 (NIV) Then they can train the younger women to love their husbands and children, to be self-controlled and pure, to be busy at home, *to be kind*, and to be subject to their husbands, so that no one will malign the word of God.

Ephesians 4:32

April 18

(Journal 1-31-2007)
    When someone asks us a question, we are faced with a choice to answer the question in a kind, gentle, humble manner, or to answer out of our pride. The first option is to simply answer the question, giving the desired response. The second response is the way of the flesh; it is cutting, sarcastic, demeaning or unkind. Pride feels repulsion in simply answering a question kindly. Pride causes us to frantically search for the best cutting response.
    We need to practice taking the path of love in responding to questions, especially at those times when we don't feel well, or when we are tired. We need to let our responses be filtered through 1 Corinthians 13.

Proverbs 31:26 (NKJV) She opens her mouth with wisdom, and on her tongue is the law of kindness.

Colossians 3:12-14
1 Corinthians 13

April 19

(Journal 2-13-2007)
 "Oh, little one, I have not stopped speaking, but you have stopped listening. You have lost many moments of comfort because you did not come to Me or because you did not open your ears to Me. I have not left you alone, yet you have deserted the One you love. I will never leave you nor forsake you. Even now My heart cries out to you, 'Draw near, draw near, revive your heart in My love, refresh your soul in My shower. Delight in the love that I have to bestow on you. Be encouraged by My nearness. Be strengthened by My delight. Rejoice in My strength.'"

2 Corinthians 1:3 (NIV) Praise be to the God and Father of our Lord Jesus Christ, the Father of compassion and the God of all comfort...

Isaiah 28:12
Hosea 14:2

April 20

(Journal 2-26-2007)
 "Ah, little one, rich is your Father toward you; rich in mercy, rich in love, rich in tender compassion. Yes, little one, delight in Me. Delight in My love for you.

Oh, little one, do not be afraid, but know that all is well. I am here to comfort. Lose yourself in Me. Gain Me as your very great reward. Do not feel like a pauper when I have given you so much. Receive freely, little one, receive freely. Enrich yourself in Me. Great is My love for you. Great is the life that I pour out upon you. In Me is life; true life."

"Spending time with You is like walking in beauty. The same wonderful, exhilarating feeling engulfs me. I am awed by Your presence, and so thankful for Your love."

"Let tenderness surround you, little one. Let My tenderness engulf you."

"There is no greater love than Yours, my Lord. Oh, great lover of my soul, there is no greater peace than the peace You give while basking in Your presence. Thank You."

Psalm 57:9-10 (NIV) I will praise you, O Lord, among the nations; I will sing of you among the peoples. For great is your love, reaching to the heavens; your faithfulness reaches to the skies.

Psalm 145:8-9
1 John 5:11

April 21

(Journal 2-27-2007)
"Rise up, little one. Rise up and praise the One who loves you. Walk in peace. All is well. Know that all is well.

How richly would I bless you, little one, if only you would open your hands to receive. My people think they are ready to receive, when their hearts are

far from Me. Draw near to Me, child. Draw near and bask in My presence. Laugh in My love."

Psalm 63:3-5 (NLT) Your unfailing love is better than life itself; how I praise you! I will praise you as long as I live, lifting up my hands to you in prayer. You satisfy me more than the richest feast. I will praise you with songs of joy.

James 4:8

April 22

(Journal 4-17-2007)
   "Walk with Me, little one. If you walk humbly, you can walk with Me."

Micah 6:8 (NIV) He has showed you, O man, what is good. And what does the LORD require of you? To act justly and to love mercy and to walk humbly with your God.

Matthew 11:29 (NIV) "Take my yoke upon you and learn from me, for I am gentle and humble in heart, and you will find rest for your souls."

Psalm 25:8-10

April 23

(Journal 5-27-2007)
   Upon leaving for church I heard: **"Come to Me, seek My face. Hold My hands and look into My face. That is where boldness and love come from. When you know**

that you are loved you can be bold, and love also. That is why I tell you, 'Come to Me before you go out.'"

(Journal 9-16-2007)
    Before leaving this morning for the Brunswick Fun Day, I held the Lord's hands and looked into His face. He poured His love into me through that spiritual contact. His love came out of me toward others the whole day. How I love being used by Him to love others. His love is so precious.

1 Chronicles 16:10-11 (NIV) Glory in his holy name; let the hearts of those who seek the LORD rejoice. Look to the LORD and his strength; seek his face always.

Psalm 27:8

April 24

(Journal 6-5-2007)
    Are we willing to do something for someone without being thanked? Are we willing to do the same thing someone else is doing, and watch the other person be recognized for his actions while we go unrecognized? Are we willing to be the unprofitable servant Jesus spoke of, the one who didn't receive a 'thank you'? God might blind others to what we have done if He detects spiritual pride in us. We need to humble our hearts and be willing to be unprofitable servants. He will lift us up in due time. But honor is not fitting for a fool (Proverbs 26:1), and we are being fools while there is spiritual pride in our hearts.
    "Thank you, Jesus, for withholding honor for our own good."

Proverbs 26:1 (NKJV) As snow in summer and rain in harvest, so honor is not fitting for a fool.

Proverbs 26:8
Luke 17:7-10

———————

April 25

(Journal 6-5-2007)
As I meditated tonight, on seeking the Lord's face, I heard in my spirit:
"What will you see,
If you look at Me?
Eyes so tender,
And a tilt of My head,
A smile on My face,
As I put you to bed."

I was given a picture in my mind of Jesus looking lovingly down at me like a father does when he puts his child to bed.
"Thank you, Jesus, for this beautiful picture."

Psalm 103:13 (NIV) As a father has compassion on his children, so the LORD has compassion on those who fear him;

Psalm 123:1-2
Psalm 4:6-8

———————

April 26

(Journal 6-25-2007)
The Lord has given me a beautiful idea for remembering to pray for people. I put a lovely basket on my bedroom floor beside my chair, filled with cards and

Christmas letters. Every prayer time, I take the front card, read it, and pray for the person or family who sent it. Their kind words help me to pray with love and fervency for them.

How I wish I had started this years ago!

Philippians 1:3-4 (NIV) I thank my God every time I remember you. In all my prayers for all of you, I always pray with joy...

Ephesians 6:18
1 Samuel 12:23
Philemon 1:4

———

April 27

(Journal 8-23-2007)
"Little one, don't you see? You could always be in connection with Me just by being thankful."

Psalm 100:4 (NIV) Enter his gates with thanksgiving and his courts with praise; give thanks to him and praise his name.

Psalm 95:2
Psalm 69:30-32
1 Thessalonians 5:16-18

———

April 28

(Journal 8-29-2007)
Tonight I took our girls and two others to a concert. While listening to the music, I told the Lord, "I want to feel Your presence." He asked me a thought provoking question:

"If you never felt My presence again, would you still love Me?" I wanted to answer, "Yes, of course!" But I had to stop and think. *Touch* was my language of love. I had felt *touched* by the Lord whenever I felt His presence. I left the concert with that question still unanswered.

I was alone in the kitchen at home when the Lord reminded me of the question. Would I love God if I never felt or heard from Him again? I realized it would be like having someone you love, away at war, separated from you by a great distance. Memories would hold you to that person. I thought of God and all that He had done in the past that showed me He loved me. I thought of what I knew about Him from His word.

The Lord had a further lesson for me. He showed me how I am to know that John loves me, based upon who he has been and what he has done. I don't need to have constant new examples in order to feel loved, or in order to love him. Jesus died for us on the cross. We love Him because of something He did for us in the past. In the same way, I am to love John for the things he has done in the past. Those things should never be erased. I don't have to base my love for John upon what he is or isn't doing for me today. My love can be based upon the truth of the past. If I anchor my love on the truth of the past, present feelings will not threaten love.

Likewise, our love for Jesus should be anchored in what He did for us on the cross, not on whether He is making us feel loved by Him right now.

Romans 5:8 (NIV) But God demonstrates his own love for us in this: While we were still sinners, Christ died for us.

Romans 8:38-39
1 John 4:19
1 Peter 1:3-9

April 29

(Journal 9-30-2007)

I told the Lord, "You used to help me more in the raising of the children."

He said, **"You haven't been praying."**

I said, "I don't mean to argue, but I've been praying a lot."

He added, **"I don't mean the little flippant prayers you throw out during the day,"** and then He spoke into my thoughts, this verse: **"The effectual, fervent prayer of a righteous man availeth much"** (James 5:16). He repeated, **"You haven't been praying."**

I realized what He meant. I hadn't been praying those fervent, down on the knees prayers—the kind where you pray until you sense a confidence that you've been heard, and that your prayers will be answered. I've been throwing out worry prayers, and worrying still, after them. Now I know why, at the end of the day, I would feel like I hadn't prayed, though reflection on the day would tell me I had.

Philippians 4:6-7 (NIV) Do not be anxious about anything, but in everything, by prayer and petition, with thanksgiving, present your requests to God. And the peace of God, which transcends all understanding, will guard your hearts and your minds in Christ Jesus.

Matthew 6:6

———————

April 30

(Journal 10-27-2007)

I must come to God, instead of trudging on ahead with my rough emotions, treading on the delicate senses of others, with impatience and inconsiderate thoughts and actions. Smiling must become a daily habit of my life.

"Oh, little one, don't neglect your time with me. In that sweet communion is where you will find sweetness of temper to carry you through the rough places of the day. Surrender your will to Me. Lay down your life. Grasp My hand and walk with Me, neither moving too quickly ahead or lagging behind. Walk with Me. I love you."

1 John 2:4-6 (NKJV) He who says, "I know Him," and does not keep His commandments, is a liar, and the truth is not in him. But whoever keeps His word, truly the love of God is perfected in him. By this we know that we are in Him. He who says he abides in Him ought himself to walk just as He walked.

John 15:4

**"My child,
a man never fails
until he gives up."**

(Journal 7-5-1985)

**"Commit this day into My hands,
your back was never meant to hold it."**

(Journal 10-7-2009)

May 1

(Journal 10-29-2007)
"Come into the room with hugs and kind words instead of with a double barrel, taking shots at people."

The Lord instructed me on this, after I had come into the kitchen this morning and immediately asked, "Who left the cookies out?" before I had even said, "Good morning" to anyone.

Philippians 4:5 (NIV) Let your gentleness be evident to all. The Lord is near.

Proverbs 16:24 (NLT) Kind words are like honey—sweet to the soul and healthy for the body.

———————————

May 2

(Journal 11-7-2007)
(Yesterday) **"You look, little one, to the comfort, love and instructions of the past, but I would desire to give you new instruction, new love and new comfort. Train your ear to listen. Train your heart to obey. I would encourage you with My love and not leave you comfortless. I love you, My child."**

(Today) **"You look to Me for answers, and that is how it should be. Do not be afraid to ask questions, but be patient for the answers. I will reveal the answers in time. Place your hand in Mine and walk with Me, little one. Know that I love you, that all is well."**

"Lord, I delight in Your presence, and breathe in the atmosphere of Your glory. I feel I'm breathing in life, just being with You."

John 14:26 (NIV) But the Counselor, the Holy Spirit, whom the Father will send in my name, will teach you all things and will remind you of everything I have said to you.

Isaiah 8:19a (NIV) When men tell you to consult mediums and spiritists, who whisper and mutter, should not a people inquire of their God?

Psalm 27:11a (NLT) Teach me how to live, O LORD. Lead me along the right path.

May 3

(Journal 4-19-2008)
"Do not fear the truth.
Speak out truth with people.
It is the lies you are to fear,
More than the truth."

Ephesians 4:25 (NIV) Therefore each of you must put off falsehood and speak truthfully to his neighbor, for we are all members of one body.

Ephesians 4:15
Colossians 3:9
Revelation 21:8

May 4

(Journal 6-27-2009)

"Ask daily, little one, if I have something to share with you, for I long to tell you many things. Do not neglect this time with Me—it is your source of power and strength.

Teach others to ask Me daily if I have something to share with them.

I long to fill you with joy daily; I long to empower you to live a godly life."

Isaiah 40:29 (NKJV) He gives power to the weak and to those who have no might He increases strength.

Psalm 68:35
Ephesians 6:10
Psalm 16:11

May 5

(Journal 7 -9-2009)

"Father, do You have a message for me today?"

"I long to tell you many things. Prepare your heart, little one. Make your heart ready to receive from Me."

"What must I do to ready my heart?"

"Your heart must be cleansed and softened, filled with love."

John 16:12 (NKJV) "I still have many things to say to you, but you cannot bear them now. However, when He, the Spirit of truth, has come, He will guide you into all truth...and He will tell you things to come."

Psalm 51:10

May 6

(Journal 8/2009)
    "Stand fast, little one. Hold to My truths. Know that I am with you and will never forsake you. Even when the sun has been darkened, and your emotions cannot be trusted, stand fast. Though the wind and the waves buffet you, stand fast. Though all around you is darkness, stand fast. Though you see no relief in sight, stand fast. I love you, and will not let you go. You will again smile. You will again feel My joy. Stand fast. I love you. Brace yourself for the long haul."

Hebrews 13:5b (NKJV) ...For He Himself has said, "I will never leave you nor forsake you."

Ephesians 6:10-17
Psalm 42

May 7

(Journal 9-2-2009)
    "My children shall receive from My heart new revelation, new understanding. As you kneel before Me, I shall open up My word to you.
    Let grace be a garland around your neck. Be engulfed in My love, enriched by My life."

"I look to You and am glad for this time."

"Little one, may your heart rejoice. Know that I love you. Reflect on all that I have done for you, and love for God will grow."

Matthew 13:12 (NLT) "To those who listen to my teaching, more understanding will be given, and they will have an abundance of knowledge. But for those who are not listening, even what little understanding they have will be taken away from them."

Deuteronomy 29:29 (NIV) The secret things belong to the LORD our God, but the things revealed belong to us and to our children forever, that we may follow all the words of this law.

Daniel 12:4 (NIV) "But you, Daniel, close up and seal the words of the scroll until the time of the end. Many will go here and there to increase knowledge."

John 16:12-15

May 8

(Journal 9-22-2009)
   "There is a difference between those who are using God, and those who are allowing God to use them."
   I heard this in my spirit after questioning the Lord about a woman I had just talked with who spoke like a Christian, but who I had never considered to be a true Christian. She said, "God has always been there for me."

Mark 10:28 (NIV) Peter said to him, "We have left everything to follow you!"

Luke 14:33 (NIV) "In the same way, any of you who does not give up everything he has cannot be my disciple."

Matthew 4:19-20 (NIV) "Come, follow me," Jesus said, "and I will make you fishers of men." At once they left their nets and followed him.

Matthew 7:21 (NIV) "Not everyone who says to me, 'Lord, Lord,' will enter the kingdom of heaven, but only he who does the will of my Father who is in heaven."

May 9

(Journal 10-10-2009)

Women who do not pray for their husbands are cutting off blessings from themselves. What affects our husbands, affects us. If we pray for blessings upon our husbands, we are praying for blessings upon ourselves, because we are 'one.' If we are angry with our husbands and refuse to pray for them, we are affecting our own health and future. Instead of feeling offended, entrust things into God's hands. He will take care of what needs to be taken care of.

Genesis 2:24 (NKJV) Therefore a man shall leave his father and mother and be joined to his wife, and they shall become one flesh.

Ephesians 5:28-33
Matthew 7:12
Jeremiah 29:7

May 10

(Journal 10-19-2009)

I learned something tonight: The longer I am on my knees speaking truth, and the closer I come into God's presence, the harder it is for demons to remain upon me with their talons sunk in. The fire of God becomes too intense for them, and they flee. I am suddenly filled with sweet peace.

No wonder demons cause us to become so restless in prayer. If they can keep us from spending much time in prayer, they can keep their foothold. The closer we get to the throne of grace the more intense the light gets, and darkness flees. When the feeling to cease praying is most intense, it is then that we most need to prevail, for we can know that we are getting closer to the light and the demons are uncomfortable.

Now, I know why some Christians, or even non-Christians, get so restless and uncomfortable while trying to pray or read the Bible. The demons are making a last-ditch effort before they are expelled. I believe this has been the reason I have sometimes felt I could not pray—could not concentrate, and why I would get up from my knees feeling agitated. I guess there is more than one way to expel a demon. They can come when we give way to anger, anxiety, stress etc.

I had begun my prayer time trusting in Jesus' message: "Come unto Me, all you who are weary and burdened and I will give you rest." (*Matthew 11:28*)

"Thank you, Jesus, for showing me this secret." (He showed me a vision of the demons on my back, loosening their grip as I approached the throne of grace. We rose like a rocket toward the kingdom of light. Finally they could not stand the intensity of God's light, His purifying fire, and they let go. This is why the Lord told me to **"Pray through it"** when spiritual darkness comes.)

Hebrews 4:16 (NKJV) Let us therefore come boldly to the throne of grace, that we may obtain mercy and find grace to help in time of need.

Ephesians 6:12

May 11

(Journal 11-17-2009)

"Father, do You have a message for me today?"

"Yes, little one. Listen to the voice of your Father. Do not be afraid to listen, little one. Do not fear that I will not speak. Rejoice in my love. Open your heart to Me, little one. Open your ears."

"Forgive me, Father, for withholding my heart from You. Forgive me for withholding my ears from You."

"Relax, little one. Know that I love you. Listen, listen to My heart. Listen to My love. Delight in My presence."

Isaiah 50:4-5 (NIV) The Sovereign LORD has given me an instructed tongue, to know the word that sustains the weary. He wakens me morning by morning, wakens my ear to listen like one being taught. The Sovereign LORD has opened my ears, and I have not been rebellious; I have not drawn back.

Proverbs 18:15 (NIV) The heart of the discerning acquires knowledge; the ears of the wise seek it out.

May 12

(Journal 11-18-2009)

"Ah, little one, My heart toward you is tender. I have been a light unto your path and will continue to

be so. **Cling to Me, little one, do not let your heart grow hardened or cold. I am your very great reward. Cling to Me.**

Refresh yourself in My love for you. Find fulfillment in My grace. I love you, little one. I will restore your heart to peace and joy. Wait on Me and you will not be disappointed. Know that I love you."

(I spent time refreshing myself in the Lord.)

Psalm 43:3-4 (NIV) Send forth your light and your truth, let them guide me; let them bring me to your holy mountain, to the place where you dwell. Then will I go to the altar of God, to God, my joy and my delight. I will praise you with the harp, O God, my God.

Psalm 103:3-5
Isaiah 40:30-31

May 13

(Journal 11-20-2009)

"Little one, your heart is weary, but I will refresh it in time. Cling to Me, little one, for My heart is tender toward you. Do you grow weary of hearing these words, but not seeing the fruit of them? Tarry still, even when your strength is low, even when your heart grows faint. Cling to Me."

"Jesus, hope deferred makes the heart sick. Strengthen me, Father, according to Your word. Help me to bear up under this weight and keep my eyes on you."

Jeremiah 31:25 (NIV) "I will refresh the weary and satisfy the faint."

Proverbs 13:12
Romans 15:13

———·•◦━━◦•·———

May 14

(Journal 12-5-2009)
 "Look to Me, little one, have I not promised to hold your hand? Know that I love you. Refreshing moments are around the corner. Do not lose hope. Times of refreshing will come.
 Know that I have in store for you everlasting treasure, everlasting joy. Not the treasure of this world, but the treasure of hearts and souls made new in Me; the only treasure that lasts for all eternity.
 My plan, little one, is to use you for My kingdom work. But first you must go through the firing process.
 Cling to Me, little one, cling to Me."

Acts 3:19 (NIV) "Repent, then, and turn to God, so that your sins may be wiped out, that times of refreshing may come from the Lord..."

Matthew 6:20

———·•◦━━◦•·———

May 15

(Journal 12-7-2009)
 The enemy comes with lies up his sleeve. He tries to make me feel that God has not been speaking to me lately, and that my life on this earth is not being profitable right now. He tries to make me feel that I am failing in everything.

Today, God showed me a picture of Satan with his hands at my throat. He is trying to take the life out of me. I started to see his lies for what they were, and I renounced them as lies and refused to believe them.

John 8:44b (NIV) "He [Satan] was a murderer from the beginning, not holding to the truth, for there is no truth in him. When he lies, he speaks his native language, for he is a liar and the father of lies."

John 10:10 (NIV) "The thief comes only to steal and kill and destroy; I have come that they may have life, and have it to the full."

James 4:7

May 16

(Journal 12-11-2009)
"Go, little one, in the love of the Lord. I will be with you and I will instruct you in what to do and say that will glorify Me. Only keep your ears open to My voice.

My children long to hear from Me, but then they go their own way and do not tune in to My Spirit. I am waiting, longing to instruct them, to encourage them, to strengthen them, but they do not lend their ears in My direction.

So seek My face, seek My voice. Be ever listening for the One who loves you."

"Oh, Jesus, tune my ears to hear Your voice in the midst of my day. Help me to recognize You, apart from the enemy, or even my own voice which can get in the way."

Nehemiah 9:20 (NLT) "You sent your good Spirit to instruct them, and you did not stop giving them manna from heaven or water for their thirst."

Proverbs 23:12

May 17

(Journal 1-4-2010)
This morning the Lord's soothing voice came into my tired spirit as He gave me an inner picture of a beautiful night sky. I heard:

> **"Walk with Me, little one.**
> **Walk with Me,**
> **To a star studded sky,**
> **Where peace and strength are symbolized**
> **By what you see.**
> **And what you see,**
> **Is but a reflection of Me.**
> **For it is My work and power**
> **That placed the stars in space.**
> **Walk with Me!"**

Genesis 5:24 (NKJV) And Enoch walked with God; and he was not, for God took him.

Psalm 102:25
Psalm 8

May 18

(Journal 1-19-2010)

"Father, I am waiting, still. Looking back on the pages of this book has been like seeing a glorious light in the darkness. It helps me cling to You, still. Reading reminded me why my face does not hold a ready smile, and why my heart is close to growing hard. Oh, Jesus, soften my heart again."

"Father, do You have a message for me?"

"When your heart grows weary and faint, look to Me, I will not fail you. Though you long for My presence and feel you are not finding it, take heart, I am near. Though the way seems weary, take heart, the sun will shine again. Though you long to see My smile and have one of your own, take heart, the time will come. Rejoice in Me, even though the feelings of rejoicement are not there. Rejoice anyway. Rejoicement will come. Ponder these things. I long to fill you with joy, but My power is being blocked. I long to stretch out My hand to heal, but right now you can't receive."

"Father, is there sin in my heart and life? What is keeping You from being able to minister to me?"

"Do not be afraid, little one. I will reveal what I need to reveal in its time. The time is not yet."

"I will trust You, Lord."

Habakkuk 3:17-18 (NIV) Though the fig tree does not bud and there are no grapes on the vines, though the olive crop fails and the fields produce no food, though there are no sheep in the pen and no cattle in the stalls, yet I will rejoice in the LORD, I will be joyful in God my Savior.

Psalm 63

May 19

(Journal 3-4-2010)
Though daily I have a peace, and an underlying joy, still there is something in the way.
"Lord, do You have a message for me today?"

"Hold fast, little one, hold fast."

"May your heart be close to Me as you bask in My presence. I would pour out understanding into your open palm. You have asked for understanding, and you shall receive. Trust Me.
I hold your hand and your life all in one mighty grasp. Be encouraged by My care."

"Hearts that desire to hear from Me will hear from Me. Hearts that long for Me will find Me."

Deuteronomy 13:4 (NIV) It is the LORD your God you must follow, and him you must revere. Keep his commands and obey him; serve him and hold fast to him.

Isaiah 26:4

May 20

(Journal 3-21-2010)
Imagine sitting with a friend and hearing yourself say, "I just don't have time to pray." Then picture yourself standing before Jesus and telling Him the same thing. Would you

suddenly remember the hour you took scanning the internet, or the half hour you took with emails or Facebook? Would you remember the novel you couldn't put down, or the movie you had to watch with your spouse or family? Would you recall the hour you spent on the phone with your best friend or relative? Maybe you would recall the time you spent poring over a magazine, working on a puzzle or a craft. Or would your face turn red as you considered the time you spent each day reading the newspaper or listening to the news. Perhaps you would consider the time you spent going out for lunch or coffee with a friend. Or would your time spent in the kitchen making desserts come to mind? Would you think about the hours you spent shopping? Maybe you would justify yourself by boasting of the hours you spent helping friends with painting and wall papering.

Let's face it. We don't spend time praying because we don't want to spend time praying, and Jesus knows it.

We will find the time to pray when we decide to seek Jesus with all our heart. And if we pray out loud we will find that we can concentrate. As we hear ourselves talking to Jesus like he's our best friend, we will suddenly realize we *love* talking to Jesus. And just about the time we realize that, we will suddenly find ourselves filled with a joy, a peace and a sense of His presence.

Just yesterday, I sensed Jesus telling me, "**You have time for all of this, but you don't have time for Me.**"

I spent a wonderful day in His presence, talking out loud, laughing, weeping, singing, praising Him and praying for myself as well as others.

Hebrews 11:6 (NIV) And without faith it is impossible to please God, because anyone who comes to him must believe that he exists and that he rewards those who earnestly seek him.

Deuteronomy 4:29

May 21

(Journal 4-30-2010)

"**Rejoice, little one, for bold is your Father on your behalf. Power resides in Me, and I show Myself powerful on behalf of My children. Do not be afraid of that which you have no control of, for I am your strong tower and refuge, a place of safety in time of trouble. I surround you with favor as with a shield. I strengthen and support you. I lift you up when you fall. I protect and deliver you, and nothing shall by any means harm you. Do I give men power to harm the body? Sometimes, but no one can harm the soul while I am its shield and defender. Look to me to defend you from all evil. I will not leave you alone. I will come when you call, and answer you quickly. Refrain from evil. Keep your tongue from evil. Then I will be bold on your behalf. Then will I clothe you with righteousness and make your garments to shine like the sun. Rejoice, little one, rejoice.**"

Psalm 9:9-10 (NIV) The LORD is a refuge for the oppressed, a stronghold in times of trouble. Those who know your name will trust in you, for you, LORD, have never forsaken those who seek you.

Psalm 5:11-12
1 Peter 3:10-12
Daniel 12:3

May 22

(Journal 5-7-2010)

"I love you, little one. I love that your heart is tender toward Me."

"Yes, little one, you need to learn and grow even in listening to Me. Do not neglect this time. The more you listen, the more you will learn. I will share things from My heart that only My listeners can know. Listen, and do not be afraid to listen.

Silence your heart before Me; still your anxious thoughts. Let My peace wash over you as you bask in My presence. Let My heart enfold you. Let My glory engulf you. Bask in Me, for in Me you will find strength. In Me you will find power. In Me you will find the desire to love and care. In Me you will find restoration. In Me you will find gladness of heart, lightness of spirit. Find in Me all that you need. My children do not have because they do not come. When they do come, they come quickly and leave quickly. They do not find what they are seeking because they do not expect to receive it. Their hearts grow wild and impatient because they will not take the time it takes to find Me. But those who wait on Me are rewarded. Those who seek Me, believing they will find Me, are blessed beyond measure.

Be one of the seekers, little one. Seek Me, wait on Me, find Me."

Every gift must be fanned into flame. I need to learn and grow in the area of listening to the Lord. I am still an infant. Just as I need to grow in the use of tongues, so do I need to grow in the use of my ears—spiritual ears.

John 6:45 (NKJV) "It is written in the prophets, 'And they shall be taught by God.' Therefore everyone who has heard and learned from the Father comes to Me."

John 10:27
Psalm 5:3

———————

May 23

(Journal 5/2010)
    "I love you too, little one.
    When you stretch out your love toward Me through a kiss blown at the ceiling, I share a tender moment with you; the greatest of lovers receiving tenderness from one so loved.
    Do not fear expressions of tenderness because you read the words of one who considers such expressions inappropriate. I am the one who determines what is and isn't appropriate. I accept and receive your tender expression with gladness of heart.
    Know that I love you; that one who loves you is near."

Luke 7:38, 44-45 (NKJV) ...and stood at His feet behind Him weeping; and she began to wash His feet with her tears, and wiped them with the hair of her head; and she kissed His feet and anointed them with the fragrant oil...Then He turned to the woman and said to Simon, "Do you see this woman? I entered your house; you gave Me no water for My feet, but she has washed My feet with her tears and wiped them with the hair of her head. You gave Me no kiss, but this woman has not ceased to kiss My feet since the time I came in."

Psalm 145:17-18

———————

May 24

(Journal 5-20-2010)
"Tune your heart to hear Me, little one. I love you and long for your presence, as you long for Mine.

I will lead you in new paths, paths your feet have not trod before. Do not be afraid, but trust in Me. My heart is tender toward you.

Continue to long for Me, little one. Continue to delight to spend time in My presence. My heart delights in you.

Know that when the shadows come I will be near you. I will not leave you comfortless. Know that when loss comes I will not leave you. Do not let your heart be sorrowful before its time. Lend your heart to Me when it is breaking, and I will hold it together. My hand will sustain you in trying times. I will be your light and your salvation. I will be the strength of your life.

Know that I am with you, that I will never leave you.

Cling to Me. Trust in Me. Rejoice in Me, and be glad all your days. When dark clouds rise, laugh them away. Find your delight in Me."

Isaiah 42:16 (NIV) "I will lead the blind by ways they have not known, along unfamiliar paths I will guide them; I will turn the darkness into light before them and make the rough places smooth. These are the things I will do; I will not forsake them."

Psalm 23:4
Psalm 73:23-26
Proverbs 31:25

May 25

(Journal 5-21-2010)
"Grow in grace, like a beautiful planting from the Lord. I have loved you. I will come to you and prune you when the time is right. Do not fear the pruning. It will only make you more beautiful if you do not chafe and twist under My loving hands. Take care that you follow My instructions. Be careful to listen and careful to act upon what I tell you.

My hand is ready to raise you up to new heights, but first you must plumb the depths. First you must be tried in the fire of suffering. Do not be afraid. Be glad in all that I have planned for you. Rejoice in your sufferings, and count your trials as joy, something to be lived out for Me."

John 15:1-2 (NIV) "I am the true vine, and my Father is the gardener. He cuts off every branch in me that bears no fruit, while every branch that does bear fruit he prunes so that it will be even more fruitful."

Isaiah 48:10
1 Peter 5:10-11
James 1:2-4

May 26

(Journal 6-7-2010)
"Trust in Me, little one. Trust that I have your good in mind no matter what the future holds. Trust in the fact that I hold your future. I will never leave you nor forsake you. I love you. My love for you is great.

I share understanding with the soul that longs for it. I share insight where insight is needed when a heart hungers for it. With you I will share My treasures of wisdom, for you have asked Me for wisdom and understanding over and over.

Rejoice in Me. Be glad in all that I will bring you."

Job 38:36 (NKJV) "Who has put wisdom in the mind? Or who has given understanding to the heart?"

Jeremiah 29:11
Hebrews 13:5
Proverbs 2:1-6
Psalm 9:2

May 27

(Journal 6-9-2010)
"Filter your thoughts through the pattern of love, 'Love is patient, love is kind...,' and you will know whether your thoughts stem from the flesh or from the Spirit."

1 Corinthians 13:4-7 (NIV) Love is patient, love is kind. It does not envy, it does not boast, it is not proud. It is not rude, it is not self-seeking, it is not easily angered, it keeps no record of wrongs. Love does not delight in evil but rejoices with the truth. It always protects, always trusts, always hopes, always perseveres.

James 3:17

May 28

(Journal 7-2-2010)

"You are climbing higher. You are not going backwards, even though it might feel like it. Your sorrow over your sin is an indication that you are climbing higher."

2 Corinthians 7:10a (NIV) Godly sorrow brings repentance that leads to salvation and leaves no regret...

May 29

(Journal 7-8-2010)

"The lover of your soul is longing for closeness with you. Bask in Me, bask in My love for you. Long for Me, as a deer pants for water. I will fill you. I will quench your thirst. I long to be to you all that you need. Place your trust in Me.

Bind your heart to Mine, and when loss comes, it will not overwhelm you. (*Tears and release.*)

Delight in Me, little one. I long to give you the desires of your heart. Establish yourself in Me. Root yourself in My word. I love you, little one."

Psalm 42:1-2 (NIV) As the deer pants for streams of water, so my soul pants for you, O God. My soul thirsts for God, for the living God. When can I go and meet with God?

Jeremiah 17:7-8
Colossians 2:6-7

May 30

(Journal 7-18-2010)
"My little one, do not put on a sour face or a sad look because of all the people who don't have what you have. I delight in your delight. Am I not able to supply their every need if they would but turn and look to Me? Could they not have what you have simply by trusting in Me, and asking? Don't beat yourself up because someone else must bear a scar. Rejoice in what I give you. Be glad in what I bring. I love to delight My children with good things. I am your Father.

Get to know the Father-heart of God. Increase your understanding. Get wisdom, get love. Where there is a lack, I will supply."

1 Timothy 6:17 (NIV) Command those who are rich in this present world not to be arrogant nor to put their hope in wealth, which is so uncertain, but to put their hope in God, *who richly provides us with everything for our enjoyment.*

Philippians 4:19
James 4:1-2
James 1:5

"Just do it.
Even if you don't feel like it,
Just do it.
Even if it's difficult,
Just do it."

———✦———

"He who has given everything to Me,
can trust Me to be everything to him."

(Journal 11-8-1986)

———✦———

June 1

(Journal 7-28-2010)
"Oh Lord, help me to not let anger and thoughtless words destroy my testimony."

"Keep apologizing to your kids along the way, when you make mistakes, thereby showing them the true gospel: 'confession and forgiveness.'"

James 5:16 (NIV) Therefore confess your sins to each other and pray for each other so that you may be healed. The prayer of a righteous man is powerful and effective.

1 John 1:9
Luke 17:3-4
Luke 24:46-48

June 2

(Journal 7-28-2010)
"Grow in grace and beauty, little one. I am here to help you as you lean on Me. Stretch out your hand to Me, for I would give you a little help. Trust Me.
Linger in My presence longer. Do not be quick to leave. Relish Me. Delight in Me. Bask in My presence. Receive My love. Be strengthened by My might."

Exodus 33:11 (NLT) Inside the Tent of Meeting, the LORD would speak to Moses face to face, as one speaks to a friend. Afterward Moses would return to the camp, but the young man who assisted him, Joshua son of Nun, would remain behind in the Tent of Meeting.

2 Peter 3:18
Luke 6:12

———————————

June 3

(Journal 8-14-2010)
"Healing is a free gift, just as salvation is."

No one says to the man seeking salvation, "Let us first see if it is God's will to forgive *all* your sins. Maybe he wants some of your sins to remain in you so that He can receive glory." No, we tell people that God can take away *all* of their sins. We give them the faith to believe, through God's word, that they are set free from *all* of their sins. None are too great to be forgiven. And yet, we do not give people the same hope when it comes to their body. We do not teach them that healing is a gift, just as salvation is a gift.

As I was praying and asking the Lord if it was true that He wanted to heal everyone, as John G. Lake seemed to stress, I heard in my spirit the phrase, **"Healing is a free gift just as salvation is."**

Jesus healed them *all*, scripture says (Matt. 12:15). Does He want to do the same for us?

John G. Lake saw salvation tied in with healing, according to Isaiah 35:4b-6a (NIV), "...he will come to save you. Then will the eyes of the blind be opened and the ears of the deaf unstopped. Then will the lame leap like a deer, and the mute tongue shout for joy."

I thought of a verse I read recently which also seems to tie in forgiveness and salvation with healing. Psalm 103:2-4 (NIV) says: "Praise the LORD, O my soul, and forget not all his benefits—who forgives all your sins and heals all your diseases, who redeems your life from the pit and crowns you with love and compassion..."

Isaiah 53:5 (NIV) But he was pierced for our transgressions, he was crushed for our iniquities; the punishment that brought us peace was upon him, and by his wounds we are healed.

1 Peter 2:24 (NIV) He himself bore our sins in his body on the tree, so that we might die to sins and live for righteousness; by his wounds you have been healed.

Matt. 4:23-24
Matthew 8:1-17
Matthew 14:35-36
Matthew 15:30
Mark 6:56
Luke 6:19
Acts 5:15-16

Note: Just as there are conditions for salvation, there are conditions for healing. Salvation and healing are not automatic or universal. Will all be healed all the time? No. God has His purposes. God also uses doctors to help bring about healing.

John G. Lake's prayer ministry brought healing, through Christ, to so many people in Spokane, WA, that "Dr. Ruthlidge of Washington, D.C., called Spokane the healthiest city in the world". 100,000 people were healed in the span of five years. (Lake, John G., *Diary of God's General.* Tulsa: Harrison House, 2004. page v)

June 4

(Journal 8-25-2010)
"Father, please forgive me for neglecting this time with You."

"Do you fear that I would leave you? I am here. I am here always, waiting for you to come to Me, waiting and longing to give you peace. Clasp your hand in Mine and walk with Me. You do not have to walk the path alone.

Do not regard yourself as 'alone' or 'lonely'; that is an affront to all that I have taught you."

Deuteronomy 31:8 (NIV) "The LORD himself goes before you and will be with you; he will never leave you nor forsake you. Do not be afraid; do not be discouraged."

Isaiah 30:18 (NLT) So the LORD must wait for you to come to him so he can show you his love and compassion. For the LORD is a faithful God. Blessed are those who wait for his help.

June 5

(Journal 8-28-2010)
After having read a portion of the book, *Touch the World Through Prayer,* by Wesley L. Duewel, I told the Lord, "I don't trust You enough." He replied, "**No, child, no one does.**"

Think of that. No one trusts God enough! 'He is able to do exceedingly abundantly more than all we ask or imagine!' (Eph. 3:20)

Numbers 20:12 (NLT) But the LORD said to Moses and Aaron, "Because you did not trust me enough to demonstrate my holiness to the people of Israel, you will not lead them into the land I am giving them!"

Isaiah 26:3-4
Proverbs 16:20

June 6

(Journal 8-30-2010)
"Be brave, and stand up under My chastisement. Do not allow your mind and heart to be led astray by discouragement or anger. Follow My plans for you. Sometimes My plans involve that which is difficult to bear, but which always holds promise of good things to come. Let your heart be stayed on Me. Learn to lean. Learn to trust even in the midst of difficulties and storms. Know that My will for you is perfect, and I will never leave you nor forsake you.

Dream your dreams, but submit them to Me. Let Me rule over all that concerns you.

Do not justify your actions or attitudes when they are displeasing to Me. Learn to submit, to bow your head under discipline. Stay your tongue."

Jeremiah 29:11 (NIV) "For I know the plans I have for you," declares the LORD, "plans to prosper you and not to harm you, plans to give you hope and a future."

Hebrews 12:5-12
Lamentations 3:22-42a
Song of Songs (Solomon) 8:5

June 7

(Journal 8-30-2010)
"Come to Me and listen, little one. Stretch out your hand to the One who loves you. Bask in My love for you.

Bask in My love for you,
Tender and sweet.
Bask in My love,

As you kneel at My feet.

Clothe yourself with My love."

Colossians 3:14 (NLT) Above all, clothe yourselves with love, which binds us all together in perfect harmony.

Romans 13:14

June 8

(Journal 9-12-2010)
"Delight yourself in Me and I will give you the desires of your heart.

Stand firm, little one, stand firm. Do not let your spirit quake within you when all is not as you think it should be; when all is not as you would like it.

I am here, and I long for you, just as you long for Me. Do not turn your eyes away from Me. Do not let your heart grow cold.

When your heart is burdened, give your burden to Me. Giving Me your burdens, does not mean just talking about them. It means handing them over and letting me take control of them. There is no peace in mere talk where your burdens are concerned.

Languish long in My presence. Delight yourself in Me; I long to fill you with pure delight."

Psalm 37:4 (NIV) Delight yourself in the LORD and he will give you the desires of your heart.

Philippians 4:1
Psalm 81:6

June 9

(Journal 9-29-2010)

   I drove home alone from Norfolk yesterday afternoon with the windows rolled down and the sun touching me. The caressing breeze and the warmth of the sun made me laugh with delight. At one point I told the Lord, "I delight in You!" A verse entered my thoughts, "Delight yourself in the Lord and He will give you the desires of your heart" (Psalm 37:4). I had been listening to praise music on the radio, which added to my joy. As the verse left my thoughts, the radio announcer said, "The Good News verse for today is, 'Delight yourself in the Lord and He will give you the desires of your heart' (Psalm 37:4)." I laughed again out of delight. It seemed the Lord was giving me a confirmation of His heart for me at that moment.

   That evening John ran a bubble bath for me. I felt loved by both him and the Lord.

John 16:27
Psalm 31:19

June 10

(Journal 9-29-2010)

   God has put within men a desire to please women.

   When a husband is met with constant criticism, complaints or dissatisfaction from his wife, he will wilt, and close up. He may give up trying to please all together, or only make attempts now and then. Some men give up sooner than others.

How do we reach a man who has given up? By letting him succeed in pleasing us—by appreciating the things he does and letting him know it, by making ourselves aware of things he does for us and being thankful.

Some things men do to please us:

- Fill up our car with gas.
- Wash the car. (He doesn't just do it for himself. But even if you *think* he is just doing it for himself, it's an opportunity to show appreciation.)
- Mow the lawn.
- Repair things around the house.
- Unclog a drain.
- Work hard at his job and bring home a pay check.
- Help with the kids.
- Help around the house.
- Make a meal. Grill.
- Get the mail.
- Take out the garbage.

For all of these are things, we can be quick to show appreciation. If we feel our husband is no longer doing these things to please us, we can imagine that he is, and thank and appreciate him as though he were. Or, we can simply appreciate his actions for what they are—he is doing something that benefits the household.

"Father, forgive me for the things my husband has done that I have failed to notice or show appreciation for. Forgive me for sometimes refusing to give him the pleasure of knowing he has pleased me. Forgive me for the times I was ungrateful and refused to be pleased because something was not the way *I* wanted it to be. Help me, Father, to remember to *often* show pleasure at what my husband has done. This makes him feel that I am pleased with *him* as a man—as my husband. I have seen my husband wilt or close-up through my displeasure. Forgive me for tearing him down instead of building him up."

The Lord showed me that Adam fell because he wanted to please his wife. That's how strong a man's desire is to please.

He also said, **"When you let him succeed in pleasing you, he will be more pleased *with* you."**

Just as our husbands need to feel that they can succeed in pleasing us, so do our children.

The day the Lord taught me about the desire he has put in men, to please women, I decided to put this knowledge into action, not only with my husband, but with my children. When I asked my son to find some hangers so I could hang up our wet laundry, he came back with one hanger. I said, "Good! You found a hanger! That will help." He seemed surprised by my pleasure. His instant response was, "I'll go find some *more*," with a lilt on the 'more', that showed his desire to please. When he returned with a bundle of hangers, his eyes flew to mine with an expectation on his face. I didn't disappoint him. I took the bundle, saying, "Thank you!" and gave him a hug. He then hung up the shirts on our downstairs clothesline without me having to ask him.

We need to let our children, as well as our husbands succeed in pleasing us.

Genesis 3:6 (NIV) When the woman saw that the fruit of the tree was good for food and pleasing to the eye, and also desirable for gaining wisdom, she took some and ate it. She also gave some to her husband, who was with her, and he ate it.

1 Kings 11:1-8

June 11

(Journal 10-1-2010)
"Let your heart rejoice, little one, for you are loved. I have loved you with an everlasting love. Long

for me, little one, long for My presence. Delight to spend time at My feet; I have much to share with you. The more often you come, the deeper I will go with you. Into this deep place of communication will I bring you, as you come to Me. Do not neglect your time with Me. I yearn for you, little one, to come into My presence on a regular basis. I long to give you so much more. I long to go deeper still. You have not even begun to know Me in the way that I desire for you to know Me. I have so much more to show you of Myself; so many mysteries for you to uncover in My word and in My presence."

Jeremiah 31:3 (NIV) The LORD appeared to us in the past, saying: "I have loved you with an everlasting love; I have drawn you with loving-kindness."

Luke 10:39 (NIV) She had a sister called Mary, who sat at the Lord's feet listening to what he said.

Jeremiah 33:3

June 12

(Journal 10-3-2010)

I prayed recently that I might be Jesus' friend again. This morning, upon waking, He reminded me of how I can be His constant companion: **"Enter into His gates with thanksgiving and into His courts with praise"** (Psalm 100:4).

I started thanking Him for people and other things. Soon I was talking with Him in prayer and feeling delight in His presence. Repentance comes first, but His gates are always open to His children if we come in by the way of thanksgiving and praise. I have known of these keys to His presence for many years, but somehow I always manage to lose them.

As my countenance changes, and my lips become upturned at the corners, I think of the long drawn faces of other Christians and I want to share with them the good news—that we can delight in God's presence by way of praise and thanksgiving. Their faces show me that bitterness, negative/critical thinking, thanklessness, resentment, self-pity, prayerlessness and lack of joy have taken up residence. I long to help them be free. But first I must establish my own freedom by the way of self-control, remembering to use the keys on a regular basis.

Give thanks for everything. This is the key.

Ephesians 5:20 (NLT) And give thanks for everything to God the Father in the name of our Lord Jesus Christ.

Psalm 118:19-20 (NLT) Open for me the gates where the righteous enter, and I will go in and thank the Lord. These gates lead to the presence of the Lord, and the godly enter there.

1 Thessalonians 5:18
Psalm 106:1
Psalm 95:2

(Note: The book *Prison to Praise* by Merlin Carothers, is a wonderful source of inspiration for remembering to be thankful.)

June 13

(Journal 10-8-2010)
The Lord has shown me that just as He has put it in men's hearts to please women, it is within His own heart to please us. He delights to please us, and is pleased when we are thankful.

Love seeks to please the other. As God seeks to please us, we also seek to please Him. Men exhibit the heart of God in their desire to please.

1 Timothy 6:17 (NIV) Command those who are rich in this present world not to be arrogant nor to put their hope in wealth, which is so uncertain, but to put their hope in *God, who richly provides us with everything for our enjoyment.*

Psalm 69:30-31
Psalm 149:3-5
Ephesians 5:10

June 14

(Journal 10-9-2010)
   "Perhaps the Lord will be silent this time."

"Would I be silent before you when you are bending your will to Mine through prayer and fasting? Will I not reach out to you with tender words of expression? I delight in you. I delight to be in your presence. When your heart is bending toward Me, and your will submissive to Mine, I delight in you. Take delight in Me.
   Broaden your scope, little one, for I desire to do new things in and through you. I long to show Myself strong on your behalf. I long to reach out to you in love, and restore your faith and confidence in Me."

(Tears of joy.) "Please restore me, Jesus."

"Return to Me, little one. Return with your whole heart to the God who loves you and longs for your friendship."

"How do I return to you, Jesus?"

"Bask in Me, delight yourself in My presence. Languish in My love. Rest in Me. Broaden your vision. All of these will restore your heart and help you to trust Me again. Time, time is of value in friendship. If you will examine what you have been investing your time in, you will realize you have often left Me out. I long for you to take great delight in My presence, to love Me above all else. You say that you do, but your actions speak differently."

"Wow, it's true, Lord. Please forgive me."

"I am calling you to a life separated unto Me. I do not call everyone to so close a tie. The plans I have for you require it. The life I have for you must be a life set apart—set apart from what others might consider a 'normal' life. I am not calling you to a 'normal life.' I am calling you to a life set apart for Me. Will you fulfill this purpose and this mission? Will you dedicate yourself to Me in a way that goes beyond the normal dedication? Will you live for Me, forsaking all else if I call you to that? Will you cleanse yourself on a regular basis, letting nothing stand between us? Will you purify yourself from all that would hinder our relationship?"

"Yes, Lord, only but help me. For I can do nothing apart from You.

Forgive me, Father, for not giving myself to You wholeheartedly. Forgive me, Father, for holding back. Forgive me for not cleansing and purifying myself from all that would hinder our relationship. I long to be used by You in mighty ways. I'm content to be used by You in little ways, if that is Your desire."

"Read only what I allow you to read, little one. Do not spend your time on books I have not called you

to. Question Me before each one. Look to Me for approval.

Do not spend time on the computer when I have not called you to it. Look to Me for permission. If it is not there, forsake that time. I will lead you.

You do not need My permission for prayer and fasting. That door is always open to you."

"Help me to live a life dedicated to You, a life following Your footsteps minute by minute, moment by moment."

"Let your words be dedicated to Me as well, little one. Speak only that which I lay upon your heart, forsaking all else. I am not calling you to 'normal' conversation. Remember, I am not calling you to a 'normal' life.

If you are to live a life set apart for Me, you need to learn to quickly and easily discern My voice. The enemy will seek to lead you astray.

You will watch on television only what I give you permission to watch. Look to Me, I will guide you.

Whenever you need guidance and direction, seek Me through prayer and fasting.

You do not need permission to speak in tongues; pray without ceasing. I will guide your tongue.

Your diet must be submitted to My control. This is a practice in listening to Me, little one. Let Me guide your eating.

The life I'm calling you to is a Spirit-controlled life."

"I submit to you, Jesus."

"Be glad in all that I am calling you to. See it not as a deprivation, but as a privilege. It is a privilege to walk hand in hand with your Savior. See in this no loss.

Call those whom I put upon your heart to call. Do not call those who I have not led you to call. Submit your calls to Me.

Submit yourself to Me, little one, in all things. Let My Spirit guide you in all things.

The Bible is open to you always."

Later on in the afternoon, I picked up the book, *On the Highroad of Surrender,* by Francis J. Roberts, and this is what I read:

Sacrifice and deprivation are nothing when they lead to a closer walk with your God. I would bring you into a place of consecration that will make possible a ministry which is beyond your present capacity. I know the way you take, and though it is now veiled to you, I am preparing the details and making ready the very things and people who will have a part in fulfilling My purposes in your life.

Psalm 4:3 (NIV) Know that the LORD has set apart the godly for himself; the LORD will hear when I call to him.

Romans 8:5-14
1 Corinthians 6:19-20
2 Corinthians 5:15

June 15

(Journal 10/2010)

"Well done, good and faithful servant. You have done well in following Me and looking to Me for guidance. Continue to submit everything to My approval. Continue to be led by My Spirit. Let My voice instruct you in the way that you should go."

"Thank you, Jesus. I love you."

"You're welcome, little one. I love you too. Be content in My love for you. Rest in My presence."

Isaiah 30:21 (NIV) Whether you turn to the right or to the left, your ears will hear a voice behind you, saying, "This is the way; walk in it."

Galatians 5:16 (NLT) So I say, let the Holy Spirit guide your lives. Then you won't be doing what your sinful nature craves.

June 16

(Journal 10-12-2010)
"If your desire is to bring glory to Me, there is no limit to what God will do through you. Those who are limited, are seeking glory for themselves. Be one who gives the praise and the glory to God. Fear receiving it for yourself."

Isaiah 26:12 (NLT) LORD, you will grant us peace; all we have accomplished is really from you.

Revelation 7:12
Acts 12:21-23

June 17

(Journal 11-12-2010)
"Hold fast, little one, to the things I have taught you. Look to Me, alone, for truth."

"Jesus, do I need your permission to pray for someone to be healed? Or do I follow the mandate, 'Freely you have received, freely give' (Matthew 10:8)? A man associated with John G. Lake's ministry out of Spokane, WA does not feel we need God's permission to heal someone. He feels it is God's desire for *all* to be made well."

"My little one, do you need My permission to bring someone to Me? You know that it is My will for all to be saved. In the same way, it is My will for all to be healed. The two go hand in hand, though My children have separated them.

I have sent you to set the captives free. My little one, set My captives free. Heal the sick, raise the dead. Bring My salvation to a fallen world. Restore what the locusts have eaten. Be My hand among My people. Stretch out your hand to heal. Work the works of God, by My Spirit."

Psalm 103:2-3 (NIV) Praise the LORD, O my soul, and forget not all his benefits—who forgives all your sins and heals all your diseases...

John 9:4 (NKJV) "I must work the works of Him who sent Me while it is day; the night is coming when no one can work."

John 14:12

June 18

(Journal 12/2010)
All of us, who have Christ in us, are lighthouses. We are to shine out Christ's light in the world, warning the world of the danger of sin which can shipwreck our lives. We shine out the beauty of our King. We show the way. We are a light set on a hill. Our job is to keep the windows of the lighthouse clean,

so His light can shine out at its brightest. We are to make sure the light in us is not veiled because of sin in our own lives.

Matthew 5:14-16 (NIV) "You are the light of the world. A city on a hill cannot be hidden. Neither do people light a lamp and put it under a bowl. Instead they put it on its stand, and it gives light to everyone in the house. In the same way, let your light shine before men, that they may see your good deeds and praise your Father in heaven."

John 8:12
2 Timothy 2:19-22
Philippians 2:14-16

June 19

(Journal 1-10-2011)

      "**You have asked a great thing. You have asked to have your mind and heart opened in understanding. I have heard you. I dish out understanding to those who ask, to those who cry out to Me as you have done. You will begin to notice a difference within the year, though it will not come all at once. You can expect a gradual unfolding which will increase as time goes by. I will light up your mind, heart and spirit, and you will begin to see things differently. I will open your ears to hear, your eyes to see and your tongue to express itself. I long to give My children good things. Simply ask.**"

Mark 4:24-25 (NLT) Then he added, "Pay close attention to what you hear. The closer you listen, the more understanding you will be given—and you will receive even more. To those who listen to my teaching, more understanding will be given. But for those who are not listening, even what little understanding they have will be taken away from them."

Proverbs 2:1-6
Matthew 7:11

June 20

(Journal 1-13-2011)
   "**May My Spirit give you understanding. May your eyes be opened by My word. May My grace be sufficient for you. May love fill your very being. May light grow brighter upon you, and may you shine out the beauty of your King.**"

Psalm 119:130 (NIV) The unfolding of your words gives light; it gives understanding to the simple.

2 Corinthians 4:6
Matthew 13:43

June 21

(Journal 1-18-2011)
   "**I always have a message for My children, little one, even if it is a message of silent love. Those who come to Me are never disappointed; not when there is a heart-felt coming and a heart-felt longing for Me. Stretch out your hand to Me, little one. I want to fill it full.**
   My children that reach out to Me are never disappointed, not when there is a true reaching from the heart. The reward is not always immediate, but it is sure."

Hebrews 11:6 (NLT) And it is impossible to please God without faith. Anyone who wants to come to him must believe that God exists and that he rewards those who sincerely seek him.

Psalm 22:5 (NIV) They cried to you and were saved; in you they trusted and were not disappointed.

June 22

(Journal 1-29-2011)

"Silent your heart before Me, little one; still your anxious thoughts. Lend your ear to the voice of My Spirit speaking to your heart. Attune yourself to My love."

"Thank You, Jesus."

"Relax in My presence. Bask in My love."

"In You is fullness of joy."

"Delight in Me, little one. Let your adoration turn into praise."

Psalm 94:18-19 (NIV) When I said, "My foot is slipping," your love, O LORD, supported me. When anxiety was great within me, your consolation brought joy to my soul.

Isaiah 30:15

June 23

(Journal 4-2-2011)
  "**All is in My hands. Trust Me to fulfill My purpose in you. Trust Me to be everything to you, to meet your every need. My children that trust Me are truly blessed. They have a wonderful heritage.**
  Develop your trust in Me, little one. Learn that I am faithful. Know Me as the one who loves you, and longs to fulfill all of your desires. When your desire is in Me, you can trust Me to fulfill your hope."

Psalm 91:2 (NIV) I will say of the LORD, "He is my refuge and my fortress, my God, in whom I trust."

Romans 15:13
Psalm 37:3-6

June 24

(Journal 4-4-2011)
  "**Find in Me your strength, little one.**"

"How do I find in You my strength, Father?"

  "**By coming to Me; by spending time in My presence. Your strength will unfold from My hand as you rest in Me. Trust Me. I love you. I know that you are weak. I do not expect you to be strong. I expect you to come to Me for strength. I expect you to need Me. When you find yourself growing weak, come to Me.**"

2 Corinthians 12:10 (NIV) That is why, for Christ's sake, I delight in weaknesses, in insults, in hardships, in persecutions, in difficulties. For when I am weak, then I am strong.

Psalm 105:4 (NIV) Look to the LORD and his strength; seek his face always.

Matthew 11:28

June 25

(Journal 4-15-2011)
"Father, how do I fan my gifts into flame?"

"By using them."

That makes sense. We shouldn't expect to be perfect in the use of our gifts; we need to exercise the use of them until they reach their full potential.

2 Timothy 1:6-7 (NIV) For this reason I remind you to fan into flame the gift of God, which is in you through the laying on of my hands. For God did not give us a spirit of timidity, but a spirit of power, of love and of self-discipline.

Ephesians 4:1-14
Romans 12:4-6
1 Timothy 4:13-15

June 26

(Journal 4-8-2011)
"The enemy would desire to beat you up, but I desire to build you up. Do not listen to the enemy of your soul. Find grace to meet your needs. I love you."

Acts 20:32 (NLT) "And now I entrust you to God and the message of his grace that is able to build you up and give you an inheritance with all those he has set apart for himself."

Ephesians 4:11-13
Ephesians 4:16
1 Thessalonians 5:11

June 27

(Journal 4-17-2011)
"Humility is God's safety valve."

Be thankful when God humbles you, he is deflating pride which would ultimately destroy you. Be thankful for humbling circumstances.

1 Timothy 3:6 (NIV) He must not be a recent convert, or he may become conceited and fall under the same judgment as the devil.

2 Chronicles 26:15-16
Proverbs 11:2
Proverbs 16:18

June 28

(Journal 5-1-2011)
I was asking the Lord to give me more emotion and feelings about things so I could pray. He said, **"When you pray I give you more emotion and feelings about**

things." Reflection showed me this was true. I wanted to be inspired to pray for people and world events, but it's while we pray that God shows us how to feel. This is one of the reasons we need to pray out of discipline, and not just when we *feel* like it.

Colossians 4:2 (NIV) Devote yourselves to prayer, being watchful and thankful.

Philippians 2:13
1 Peter 4:7

June 29 & 30

(Journal 5-7-2011)
    "Learn to trust Me more and more. Let your delight be in Me. I love you. I love you, not merely in words, but with every beautiful sunset I parade before your eyes; with every beautiful song I let enter your ears. I love you through the voice of others; I love you through their touch."

Psalm 136

**"True humility
is recognizing the source of your gifts."**

Humility lets others have the last word.

July 1

(Journal 5-19-2011)
   "Let your heart grow closer to Me. Find in Me your strength. Find in Me your laughter. There is no reason to be lonely when I am here.
   Bask in My love for you. Bring Me your cares and fears. Find in Me the friend you seek. Let Me restore you to a place of fellowship beyond normal understanding. Delight yourself in Me, and I will delight in you.
   Take a bath, little one. Come and find rest for your soul. Reflect upon My love for you. Drink deeply of My rest."

Psalm 23:2b-3a (NIV) ...he leads me beside quiet waters, he restores my soul.

Psalm 62:5 (NIV) Find rest, O my soul, in God alone; my hope comes from him.

July 2

(Journal 5-23-2011)
   It is God's tender mercy that He shows us our sins little by little. During a revival, He opens the flood gates and people are confronted with their sins in full force. That is why they weep and wail. The impact on their emotions is great.
   When God deals with a heart gradually, it is no less significant; the outcome is what matters.
   (The Lord showed me this as I wept over my sin.)
   When we spend time with Him on a regular basis, He has time to deal with our sins little by little. It is His mercy that we are not overwhelmed.

Hebrews 5:2 (NIV) He is able to deal gently with those who are ignorant and are going astray, since he himself is subject to weakness.

Psalm 32:1-5

July 3

(Journal 5-30-2011)

"Grow in grace, little one. Find in Me your all in all. As I release you to serve Me in greater capacities, find in Me your strength, your help, your love, your encouragement. Stand tall in Me. When the enemy strikes, stand firm. I have given you victory over the enemy. Know your place, know your authority."

Luke 10:19 (NIV) "I have given you authority to trample on snakes and scorpions and to overcome all the power of the enemy; nothing will harm you."

Ephesians 6:10-18

July 4

(Journal 6-11-2011)

As I was praying for the people involved in the Chili earthquake, I sensed the Lord telling me, **"Earthquakes are a warning for people to build their lives on the 'Rock.'"**

Matthew 7:24 (NIV) "Therefore everyone who hears these words of mine and puts them into practice is like a wise man who built his house on the rock."

Isaiah 44:8
1 Corinthians 10:2-5
Luke 13:2-5

July 5

(Journal 6-12-2011)
    I just read Ezekiel 22:30-31, from the NLT Bible: "*I looked for someone who might rebuild the wall of righteousness that guards the land. I searched for someone to stand in the gap in the wall so I wouldn't have to destroy the land, but I found no one. So now I will pour out my fury on them, consuming them with the fire of my anger. I will heap on their heads the full penalty for all their sins. I, the Sovereign LORD, have spoken!*"
    With tears filling my eyes I cried, "Here am I, send Me!" It is the wall of righteousness that guards our land from God's fury. This wall is being destroyed in our nation even now.
    "Oh, Jesus, help us to be builders of that wall. Oh, Jesus, help our children to be builders of that righteousness."
    "How do we rebuild the wall, Father?"
    I feel like Nehemiah, weeping in his heart before the king. The wall must be rebuilt, but how?
    "I pray that you would put it upon the hearts of others to stand in the gap, to rebuild this wall of righteousness in our nation.
    Help us to fix 'broken windows' and broken walls." (John's sermon for today was about the 'broken windows' theory that was brought out at General Council through a seminar.)
    The Lord spoke these words:

"Are you willing to take insult and persecution? Are you willing to stand up for what is right and be blamed or accused of wrong doing? Are you willing to lay down your reputation for My sake? Are you willing to stand condemned? Are you willing to have the filth of the world flung at you? Are you willing to defeat the enemy on his own turf?

Then stand up and be counted, for I will surely use a man like that."

Isaiah 6:8
Acts 24:24-27
Ephesians 5:1-6
Matthew 5:10-12

July 6

(Journal 6/2011)
"Do not fear, little one. You have allowed fear to take over your thoughts."

"Trust in Me, little one. Trust that I want to meet your needs, and the needs of others that you pray for. Give your heart to Me, little one. Let it rest in My hands, I will take good care of it. I make all things new. Anything entrusted into My care will not remain unchanged. I will enlarge your heart. I will quicken your heart. I will strengthen your heart."

Psalm 28:7 (NIV) The LORD is my strength and my shield; my heart trusts in him, and I am helped. My heart leaps for joy and I will give thanks to him in song.

John 14:27

July 7

(Journal 6-2-2011)

"Take heart, little one, take heart. Allow your thoughts to rest on Me. In this you will find comfort, in this you will find strength. I will give you insight and understanding. I will give you what you seek.

Seek to know My will. Seek to walk in holiness and godliness.

I will teach you, little one. I will instruct you in the way that you should go. Trust Me."

Romans 12:1-2 (NIV) Therefore, I urge you, brothers, in view of God's mercy, to offer your bodies as living sacrifices, holy and pleasing to God—this is your spiritual act of worship. Do not conform any longer to the pattern of this world, but be transformed by the renewing of your mind. Then you will be able to test and approve what God's will is—his good, pleasing and perfect will.

2 Peter 3:11
Psalm 25:4-5

July 8

(Journal 7-6-2011)

"Walk in belief, little one. Believe that I *want* to speak to you. To walk in unbelief is to walk as an unbeliever. You have chosen to walk in unbelief at times. You have chosen to close your ears to My voice when all along I am calling out to you to 'listen'. You have closed up your ears out of fear and chosen to ignore My pleading.

As I call to you, little one, open your ears. Trust Me. Trust the One who loves you. Examine the message, examine the Spirit behind it. Test everything. Learn to know the true from the false, but do not close your ears out of fear.

I will heal your heart, little one. I will revive you to walk in My Spirit."

Revelation 2:7 (NIV) He who has an ear, let him hear what the Spirit says to the churches. To him who overcomes, I will give the right to eat from the tree of life, which is in the paradise of God.

1 John 4:1-3
1 Thessalonians 5:20-21

July 9

(Journal 7-8-2011)
"Hear the voice of your Shepherd. Know that I am longing to lead you to pleasant pastures. I long to refresh your soul in Me. Be one who is easily led."

Psalm 32:9 (NIV) Do not be like the horse or the mule, which have no understanding but must be controlled by bit and bridle or they will not come to you.

Psalm 23

July 10

(Journal 7-11-2011)

"Grow in grace, little one. My eyes are always upon you. Trust Me; know that I am God. Stand your ground when the enemy attacks. You are precious in My sight. I delight in you. The enemy may be strong, but in Me, you are stronger. Take delight in the challenges set before you. Take delight in Me. Know that I love you, that My hand is upon you. When the storm rages around you, stand firm. You are the apple of My eye. Rejoice in My love for you."

Psalm 46:10 (NLT) "Be still, and know that I am God! I will be honored by every nation. I will be honored throughout the world."

Psalm 17:6-9

———

July 11

(Journal 9-2-2011)

"Learn to discern the true from the false. I will lead you into all truth. Clasp My hand, little one. Clasp it in yours and hold it tight. I will lead you, but the way may be a rocky way. As you climb the heights, the path may grow steep, but My hand will guide you. I will bring you to safety and you shall rejoice in Me.

Reach up to Me, little one, and I will lift you up. Find your joy in Me. Traverse the heights with Me. Enjoy the beauty of the world from this height, but know that I am God and I will give My glory to no other.

I long to lead you into deeper truths. Prepare your heart to receive."

John 16:13 (NIV) "But when he, the Spirit of truth, comes, he will guide you into all truth. He will not speak on his own; he will speak only what he hears, and he will tell you what is yet to come."

Psalm 143:10 (NLT) Teach me to do your will, for you are my God. May your gracious Spirit lead me forward on a firm footing.

James 4:10 (NIV) Humble yourselves before the Lord, and he will lift you up.

July 12

(Journal 10-8-2011)

Again, this Autumn, I was having a miserable time with allergies. Somehow I forgot all about thanking and praising the Lord, and praying for people, cities and countries with my allergy symptoms. But low and behold, when I started the pattern of praise and prayer with every symptom, my symptoms once again went away; with the exception of sneezing in the morning and again at night. But this allowed me to change the letters of the alphabet. What an amazing God we have, who teaches us amazing things.

1 Chronicles 23:30 (NIV) They were also to stand every morning to thank and praise the LORD. They were to do the same in the evening...

Psalm 47:2
Hebrews 13:15

July 13

(Journal 10-17-2011)

"There are some things that only come with time in My presence. The power to live a godly life is one of those.

Spend time in prayer before you spend time in reading, little one. After you have made that connection with Me in the Spirit realm, I can teach you through My word." (I often get so caught up in reading and studying scripture, that I lose my time for focused prayer.)

"...those who live apart from Me lead a frustrated life. They cannot succeed in what they attempt to do though they know what I require of them. I desire for all of My children to walk in power, but there are no shortcuts. Time with Me is essential.

Whenever you see a Christian whose eyes and countenance have dimmed, you know that you are looking at a man or woman who is working without prayer.

I have had grace toward you, little one; I have not allowed you to succeed without prayer. Those who succeed through self-effort fall to their destruction." (Unless the LORD builds the house, those who build it labor in vain. Psalm 127:1a)

"When you find that the source of inspiration for all work has dried up, then you can know you have not been spending time in My presence. I am the source of all inspiration. When visions have died and dreams are rare, know that you have wandered away from the source of all inspiration. You have wandered on through the dry seasons without acknowledging My absence."

There are different levels to spending time in God's presence just as there are different levels of inspiration. Sometimes we are content on the surface level when God would take us deeper.

John 15:1-8
Galatians 5:22-23

July 14

(Journal 11-3-2011)

"Grow in grace, little one. Your time to grow is now. Stretch out your hand to Me, that I may restore you. Lose yourself in Me. I am your strong tower. I am your shield of defense. I am the one who loves you with an everlasting love. I am the one who delights in you. I am the one whose eyes are always upon you to bring you good and not harm. Rejoice, little one, rejoice.

Long for Me. Little one. Delight yourself in Me and I will give you the desires of your heart. Delight in Me."

Later: "Open your eyes, little one, to My love. It is all around you. How I love to delight My children through nature."

Psalm 144:2 (NIV) He is my loving God and my fortress, my stronghold and my deliverer, my shield, in whom I take refuge, who subdues peoples under me.

Psalm 33:5-9

July 15

(Journal 12-16-2011)
    "Return to Me, little one, and I will return to you. Draw near to Me, and I will draw near to you. You might ask, 'How can I be spending time with You and yet not be near you?' Return with your *whole* heart. I long to be everything to you, but first I need everything *from* you."

    "What am I holding back from You, Jesus? Search my heart, Lord."

    "I would desire for you to pour out your heart before Me, but you have held it in reserve. We are not on the intimate level we once shared. You have closed off your heart to Me and I have not been your confidante. Return to Me, little one. Find in Me the close friend you desire. Pour out your heart to Me. I will be all you need."

Zechariah 1:3 (NIV) "Therefore tell the people: This is what the LORD Almighty says: 'Return to me,' declares the LORD Almighty, 'and I will return to you,' says the LORD Almighty."

Psalm 62:8

———

July 16

(Journal 12-29-2011)
    "If you choose to listen, I will speak. If you choose to speak, I will listen."

    (I had apologized to the Lord for interrupting Him and taking the conversation in a different direction. He is a gentleman; if we talk, He will listen, but it will be our loss.)

*Calvin Miller writes: "*When you open up the Bible and you pray the scriptures back to God, you're experiencing something wonderful...He's delighted...We are talking and God is listening. But the best times are when God starts talking, and we're quiet enough to hear him.*"

Psalm 34:6 (NLT) "In my desperation I prayed, and the LORD listened; he saved me from all my troubles."

Psalm 34:11 (NIV) Come, my children, listen to me; I will teach you the fear of the LORD.

*Calvin Miller's quote is taken from *Be Still and Know that I am God Promise Journal*. Ellie Claire Gifts and Paper Corp. Minneapolis.

———————

July 17

(Journal 1-28-2012)
"Stand fast, little one. Your light is about to grow brighter. I am your light. I will enrich you as you spend time with Me. Know that I love you. Know that I care about all that concerns you. My grace is sufficient for you.

Pray to overcome. Pray to stand fast. Release My power into your life through prayer. Do not leave this resource untapped. I have much to give you if you will claim it from Me. It is your right as My child."

John 8:12 (NIV) When Jesus spoke again to the people, he said, "I am the light of the world. Whoever follows me will never walk in darkness, but will have the light of life."

2 Corinthians 12:9
Proverbs 4:18

July 18

(Journal 3-29-2012)

Genesis 18:12 (NLT) So she laughed silently to herself and said, "How could a worn-out woman like me enjoy such pleasure, especially when my master—my husband—is also so old?"

Sarah, laughing to herself about having a baby in her nineties, is a good example for us to take seriously what we think in our heart. She said she had *not* laughed because she only laughed silently to herself. But the Lord said she *did* laugh.

Do we scorn or criticize something in our thoughts but disguise our spoken words with kindness, thinking we do well because we do not speak out loud unkindly? I'm beginning to understand how God is concerned with what is in our heart.

God considered Sarah's laughing thoughts as serious as if she had laughed audibly. We need to repent of our thoughts, and be careful about where we let them go.

"Forgive me, Father, for all the wrong things I have allowed my mind to think through the years."

Proverbs 23:7 (NKJV) For as he thinks in his heart, so is he: "Eat and drink!" he says to you; but his heart is not with you.

2 Corinthians 10:5
Philippians 4:8

July 19

(Journal 4-7-2012)
    "**Embrace My love for you. Feel My presence and My peace. I love you, My child. You long for Me, and I long to give you what you long for. I long to give you the desires of your heart.**

    In Me lie all the treasures of wisdom; receive from Me. Find in Me your great reward.

    I delight in you, little one, as you delight in Me. Hold Me close to your heart, for I am holding you."

Colossians 2:2-3 (NIV) My purpose is that they may be encouraged in heart and united in love, so that they may have the full riches of complete understanding, in order that they may know the mystery of God, namely, Christ, in whom are hidden all the treasures of wisdom and knowledge.

Jude 1:1-2
Psalm 37:4

July 20

(Journal 4-8-2012) Easter
    "**Rise up, little one. Rise above your problems, your struggles, your questions, and trust in Me. Lay aside all that hinders you from coming to Me in confidence. Know that I am waiting for you and ready to receive you just where you are. My heart is open to you. I do not demand hard things of you. You have made them difficult with your indecision and disobedience. Train yourself to obey, and joy will be yours. Follow me; I long to lead you.**"

1 Timothy 4:7 (NIV) Have nothing to do with godless myths and old wives' tales; rather, *train yourself* to be godly.

1 John 3:21-24
John 15:10-11

July 21

(Journal 4-9-2012)
    "Let My heart enfold you. Do not be afraid of all I set before you. I am calling you to a path that not everyone can walk, but only those who truly desire to do My will. You will be stretched to your limits, but you will rejoice to be following Me. You never walk alone. I never call My children to more than they can bear. Trust Me. Know that I love you."

Luke 5:27-28 (NIV) After this, Jesus went out and saw a tax collector by the name of Levi sitting at his tax booth. "Follow me," Jesus said to him, and Levi got up, left everything and followed him.

Psalm 73:23-24

July 22

(Journal 4-10-2012)
    "Do you long for My presence with all your heart? Do you seek to know Me better and yearn to be the first one up, waiting at the feet of your Lord? What happened to hinder you, little one? When did you cease making Me the top priority of your life? When did you start feeling you could live your life apart from Me? Return to Me, little one. I wait with

open arms. Do not neglect your time with Me. Bask in My presence, bask in My love."

Isaiah 30:15 (NLT) This is what the Sovereign LORD, the Holy One of Israel, says: "Only in returning to me and resting in me will you be saved. In quietness and confidence is your strength. But you would have none of it."

Isaiah 44:22
Malachi 3:7

July 23

(Journal 4/2012)
   "Oh, My little one, I hear the cry of your heart, that your desire is to please Me. I know that you long to draw closer to Me in intimacy. I am working on your behalf to make this possible. I know that you are longing to pray without ceasing. So shall I strengthen you on this behalf. You will glorify Me, and I will be pleased with your progress."

Ephesians 5:10 (NIV) ...and find out what pleases the Lord.

1 Thessalonians 5:17

July 24

(Journal 4/2012)
   "Open your palms to Me, little one. Find in Me the fulfillment of everything you need. I will pour into your open palms the blessing of My presence as you

look to Me to supply the grace to meet every situation. I love you. I long for you to draw continually closer. Know that I am with you. I fill you with My life. Out of your belly shall flow rivers of living water."

John 7:38 (KJV) "He that believeth on me, as the scripture hath said, out of his belly shall flow rivers of living water."

Psalm 28:2
Psalm 63:3-5

July 25

(Journal 4/2012)
 "Thank You, Jesus, that You are our Shepherd. You are caring for us. We do not need to fear evil. All is in Your hands."

 If the Lord is our Shepherd, can anything happen to us that He is not aware of? We are under His watchful eye as long as we stay close to Him. If we wander off, away from Him, then anything He allows to happen to us serves the purpose of drawing us back to His side.

 "Thank You, Jesus!"

John 10:14 (NIV) "I am the good shepherd; I know my sheep and my sheep know me—"

John 10:27-28
Psalm 23

July 26

(Journal 4/2012)

"I always have a message for you, little one. In the midst of a busy day you can still find Me as you kneel, seeking My closeness. Do not let the enemy distract you from spending time with Me. Long for Me, and I will fulfill your desire. Rest in Me. Breathe deep, and let My Spirit give you peace. Cling to Me. Find your strength in Me."

Psalm 29:11 (NIV) The LORD gives strength to his people; the LORD blesses his people with peace.

1 Chronicles 28:9 (NLT) "And Solomon, my son, learn to know the God of your ancestors intimately. Worship and serve him with your whole heart and a willing mind. For the LORD sees every heart and knows every plan and thought. If you seek him, you will find him. But if you forsake him, he will reject you forever."

July 27

(Journal 4-14-2012)

"Cling to Me harder. Cling to Me still, in moments of confusion. I will never leave you nor forsake you. Know that in Me, all is well. If you are living in My presence you will not walk in chaos. I will order your steps aright. You will find in Me a solid footing. I delight to lead you, only delight to follow, little one, and your life will be full. I have come to give you abundant life. Live in Me."

Jeremiah 10:23 (NIV) I know, O LORD, that a man's life is not his own; it is not for man to direct his steps.

Psalm 16:11
Proverbs 3:6

July 28

(Journal 4/2012)
"My heart is gracious toward you. Know that I love you. I will never leave you alone. When all is dark and still, know that the light is shining very near you. Just reach out your hand and I am there. Like the sun hiding behind the clouds, I am ever near. Know that darkness can never extinguish My love from you.
Cling to Me, little one. Cling to Me."

Romans 8:35-39 (NIV) Who shall separate us from the love of Christ? Shall trouble or hardship or persecution or famine or nakedness or danger or sword? As it is written: "For your sake we face death all day long; we are considered as sheep to be slaughtered." No, in all these things we are more than conquerors through him who loved us. For I am convinced that neither death nor life, neither angels nor demons, neither the present nor the future, nor any powers, neither height nor depth, nor anything else in all creation, will be able to separate us from the love of God that is in Christ Jesus our Lord.

Psalm 18:28
Psalm 145:18

July 29

(Journal 4-25-2012)

This thought from the Lord, came to me upon waking, concerning Satan:

"...and he comes like one wanting to bring relief."

Satan comes to people with the temptation toward alcohol, drugs, pornography, adultery, and other addictions under the guise of bringing relief from stress, trouble, a poor marriage relationship, etc.

Psalm 4:1 (NIV) Answer me when I call to you, O my righteous God. Give me relief from my distress; be merciful to me and hear my prayer.

Psalm 46:1 (NIV) God is our refuge and strength, an ever-present help in trouble.

1 Corinthians 10:13
Mark 14:38
Hebrews 2:18

July 30

(Journal 5/2012)

"Messages come in many ways, little one. To some I speak directly in their spirits, to others I speak plainly in their ears, to some I speak through circumstances..."

Acts 10:13-20 (NLT) Then a voice said to him, "Get up, Peter; kill and eat them." "No, Lord," Peter declared. "I have never eaten anything that our Jewish laws have declared impure and unclean." But the voice spoke again: "Do not call something unclean if God has made it clean." The same vision was repeated three times. Then the sheet was suddenly pulled up to heaven. Peter was very perplexed. What could the vision mean? Just then the men sent by Cornelius found Simon's house. Standing outside the gate, they asked if a man named Simon Peter was staying there. Meanwhile, as Peter was puzzling over the vision, the Holy Spirit said to him, "Three men have come looking for you. Get up, go downstairs, and go with them without hesitation. Don't worry, for I have sent them."

Acts 9:4-7
Job 33:14-30

July 31

(Journal 5-24-2012)
"Learn to trust Me more and more. I have only your good in mind, and I love you beyond what you can imagine. My love for you is expressed in so many ways. Learn to recognize it on a moment by moment basis. It is all around you, whether it is the light you see or the air you breathe. If you recognize My love in these things and more, you will always feel hugged— embraced by My love. I love you, Laura."

Psalm 26:3 (NLT) For I am always aware of your unfailing love, and I have lived according to your truth.

Psalm 42:8
Psalm 119:64

"Worry, stress and fear
are the calling cards of the enemy;
reject them."

———————

"Focus on what you feel glad about
rather than what you feel bad about."

———————

August 1

(Journal 6-3-2012)

"Relax, and rest in My presence. I love you. I will be strong on your behalf if you continually look to Me. Why do I need to tell My children so often to look to Me? Because they allow many things to come between us. Their gaze is not fixed on Me. If it were, they would experience perfect peace. Do you have perfect peace, little one? If not, ask yourself, 'What is standing between me and God?'"

Isaiah 26:3 (NKJV) You will keep him in perfect peace, whose mind is stayed on you, because he trusts in you.

Psalm 105:4
Hebrews 12:2-3

August 2

(Journal 6-12-2012)

"Take heart, little one, the Father loves you. As you long for Him, He longs for you to come closer. I love you, My child. Rejoice and rest in My love. Joy and peace I give you. Let not your heart be troubled, neither let it be afraid. Long for Me, little one, as you longed for Me last night. To be homesick for heaven is to be homesick for Me."

John 14:27 (NIV) "Peace I leave with you; my peace I give you. I do not give to you as the world gives. Do not let your hearts be troubled and do not be afraid."

Psalm 90:1-2 (NLT) Lord, through all the generations you have been our home! Before the mountains were born, before you gave birth to the earth and the world, from beginning to end, you are God.

John 14:23
Colossians 3:1-4

August 3

(Journal 6/2012)
"Listen, little one, and I will always share My heart with you because I love you. I have a message for you in your deepest darkest moments and I have a message for you in your brightest moments. Listen, for I love you."

John 6:45 (NIV) "It is written in the Prophets: 'They will all be taught by God.' Everyone who listens to the Father and learns from him comes to me."

Isaiah 51:1
1 Samuel 3:9

August 4

(Journal 7-5-2012)
"Make it your ambition in Life to spend time listening to Me. Set your ear to hear and your heart to obey. I have so much to share with you, little one, if you will only set apart that time with Me. I love you. I stretch out My hand to you often, but you do not take it. I desire to minister to you but you leave My words unheard. Find strength in Me, little one. Restore the

fellowship we once knew—and go beyond to discover new depths you have never known. Oh, rejoice in Me, little one, for I delight in you. I look forward to this time with you as you set your heart to listen. Seek and you will find. You have been seeking a deeper relationship with Me, yet you have neglected to listen to Me on a regular basis."

"Oh, Lord, I set my heart to hear You. I set my heart to feel and know You. I set my heart to rejoice in You. Help me to follow hard after You. Forgive me for my negligence."

As I watched a robin from our back yard step, I heard the Lord say, **"Oh, little one, I have new beauties to show you; new delights to give you. Stretch out your hand to Me and receive all that I desire to bring you.**

You have missed the Spring, but you shall know the Summer in My presence. Learn and grow. Receive and bless, for I desire that you shall be a blessing through what you receive from Me.

Do you see the sun sinking low? It's beauty shall be seen for a few more hours. Relish all that I give you through nature.

You shall have to get notebooks, for you shall fill them up with all I share with you. Take time to listen. Take time to love Me. Take time to laugh in My presence and delight yourself in Me. I love you, little one."

"I just realized, the notebooks will be filled up, not just with Your words, but with poems and stories from Your heart! These are some of the treasures You desire to share with me as I spend time in Your presence. I love You, Father."

"Rest in Me, little one. The night will soon be falling and darkness will enfold you. Even in the presence of the night you can enjoy My presence.

Let My words not fall on deaf ears, but come to Me with an open heart, an open ear, a desire to learn, to receive from Me all I long to give you."

"Thank You, Jesus."

(Later) "Stand tall, little one. I have called you to bear My name. I have called you to be a light to those in darkness. Do not be afraid of them, but stretch out your hand in love. I will use you to bless others. I will use you to turn the sinner from his ways. Your eyes will no longer be red from weeping for those you feel you cannot affect in your own strength. No, for you shall walk in mine and I shall go before you. Stand tall. Rejoice in Me, for if you remain in My love you shall do far more than you have imagined. Only live in Me, walk in Me, move and breathe in Me and do not let go of My hand."

Psalm 78:1 (NLT) O my people, listen to my instructions; open your ears to what I am saying.

John 15:4 (NIV) "Remain in me, and I will remain in you. No branch can bear fruit by itself; it must remain in the vine. Neither can you bear fruit unless you remain in me."

Deuteronomy 6:5

August 5

(Journal 7-6-2012)
"Good morning, little one. As you start the day with Me, let Me awaken within you desire; desire to hear, desire to listen, desire to understand and receive. Bask in My love. Let My love engulf you.

Know Me, little one, know Me. Let My Spirit make you glad:
Glad, for the day is just beginning.
Glad, because I have given you, life.
Glad, because I love you.
Glad, because you love Me."

"Listen to Me, little one, all through the day, and you will receive much joy."

"Thank You, for letting us come into Your presence because of Jesus, who has made us clean and right before God."

"Draw near, little one, draw near. I will teach you many things, and bring all things to your remembrance, whatever I have told you.
Relish your time with Me. Let it be a joy and a delight. Let it feed your soul and nourish your mind and heart. I love you."

(Later) "Enter into My presence. Know the joy of My fellowship. Listen, little one, listen with your heart, for that is where I reside. Let your love for Me grow fonder. Enjoy Me, by enjoying the world I created."
(I'm sitting out on the back step. There are wild bunnies playing close by, birds flying back and forth, and the sun is preparing to set behind some hazy clouds. A gentle breeze is keeping me cooler in this ninety degree weather. I am glad to be here.)
"Saturate your mind with thoughts of Me, for truly I long to be everything to you. In Me is everything you need. Rest in Me, little one, rest in My presence. Soon I will call you to work in My presence, but tonight just rest in Me."
(The sun is setting with a brilliant pink/orange color. The green fields and smoky looking trees mixed with forest green, look so lovely on the horizon.)

"Learn to love Me through what you see, for what you see is a reflection of Me. All of My handiwork is given in love."

"Pray for your neighbor, little one." (Our neighbor just came out to his grill.)

Isaiah 61:10 (NIV) I delight greatly in the LORD; my soul rejoices in my God. For he has clothed me with garments of salvation and arrayed me in a robe of righteousness, as a bridegroom adorns his head like a priest, and as a bride adorns herself with her jewels.

Romans 1:19-20
Psalm 145

August 6

(Journal 7-7-2012)
"Stay in tune with Me. Let your soul rejoice in My presence. Find delight in the sound of the birds. Listen to the sounds of summer.

Stand firm, little one—clothed in My Spirit, rescued from the evil one, set free and delivered, anointed to serve, filled with My love."

"Let My love be a gift to you, little one, that you unwrap with delicacy. Let it be a sweet joy, exploding in myriads of colors like a magnificent fireworks display. So shall I delight your senses."

"Thank You, Jesus. I receive Your love."

"I delight in delighting you."

"Oh, little one, you shall not begin to capture all that I plan for you, all that I desire to delight you with, but try, little one. Try to put into words the love I express to you in the myriads of ways I choose to delight you. Capture some of it, and share that delight with the world. Perhaps some will be drawn to Me because of My love for you, and your love for Me."

"Thank You for the pleasures You long to give us, even now, on this earth. Thank You, Jesus."

Psalm 97

August 7

(Journal 7-11-2012)
"Forgive me; how quickly I get too busy to listen."

"Cleanse your heart from all that hinders you from hearing Me, all that hinders you from listening. Take time to sit in My presence and delight in Me."

The sun is warm upon me. The sound of the air conditioner beside me is drowning out the sounds of summer, except for the birds and a distant dog. But the air conditioner is a promise of cool relief when I leave these back steps.

I just read Psalm 107:8 (NKJV), "Oh that men would give thanks to the Lord for his goodness, and for his wonderful works to the children of men!" Verses 15, 21, and 31 all say the same thing. And so I say, "Thank You, Jesus! Thank You for the beauty and warmth of the sun! Thank You for this time in Your presence. Thank You for the meeting tonight."

"I long to give you more. Let My life be made manifest to you as you rejoice in Me. Know Me in the beauty of holiness. Know My love for you. Know My delight. Receive all that I long to give you. Trust in Me and relinquish yourself to Me.

Bless you, little one. My blessing I bestow upon you. Find strength. Find peace."

"Lord, I receive strength and peace at Your hand. I delight in You, and my soul is glad."

Psalm 107

August 8

(Journal 7-13-2012)
"Clasp your hand in Mine, little one. Walk with Me, rest in Me, enjoy My presence."

"Help me to know and love You, Jesus."

"Wave upon wave, wave upon wave, restless, unending, enduring it seems. Imagine your life as a wave, little one, etching the edge of the sands of time. I have brought you into existence for a purpose. Your life is meant to leave a mark, to make a difference, to change the face of humanity. Every life who follows Mine is meant to carve out a change. The world should not look the same because you have been here. Sense the beauty of your purpose. Clothed in Christ, you make an indelible impression upon society. You leave it shifted from its former complacency.

Walk with Me, little one, walk with Me along the sands of time and see the earth being changed by My existence.

You are here for a little while. Only I can make your life count for something while you are on this earth. Look to Me to create the story. Look to Me to bring out the beauty of your existence. Clothed in Me you have a purpose.

Come, little one, take My hand and walk with Me."

Isaiah 48:18 (NKJV) Oh, that you had heeded my commandments! Then your peace would have been like a river, and your righteousness like the waves of the sea.

Psalm 89:15
Galatians 3:27

August 9

(Journal 7-15-2012)
"**Draw near, draw near.**
> **Capture My heart for you**
> **as you link your heart with Mine.**

Draw close, draw closer still.
> **Quiet your heart before Me**
> **and let Me fill you with My life.**
> **I will fill you to overflowing.**

Capture My heart for you,
Capture the essence of My love.
> **Feast upon the richness**
> **of all that I have prepared for you.**

Draw close, draw closer still.
> **Delight yourself in Me.**
> **Yield yourself to Me.**

Unclasp your hands from all
> **that would pull you away from Me.**
Spend your time delighting in Me,
> **And I shall give you the desire of your heart.**
Minister to Me and let Me minister to you.

Let My life be reflected in your face.
    You are My jewel,
    My precious reflection of My love.
You shall shine for Me.
    You are My delight.
    Awaken your heart to love Me.

Blessings,
Blessings upon you, little one."

Zechariah 9:16 (NLT) On that day the LORD their God will rescue his people, just as a shepherd rescues his sheep. They will sparkle in his land like jewels in a crown.

2 Corinthians 3:18 (NLT) So all of us who have had that veil removed can see and reflect the glory of the Lord. And the Lord—who is the Spirit—makes us more and more like him as we are changed into his glorious image.

Psalm 135:1-4

August 10

(Journal 7-18-2012)
    "Trust in Me, little one. Trust in My love for you. Surrender your heart to Me on a regular basis, as you have been doing. A surrendered heart is a heart that I can use. Never grow weary of surrendering yourself, thinking that it is just a ritual. It is your lifeline to Me. It is your invitation for Me to use you.
    Live in the afterglow of My love as I extend Myself to others through you. When you bless others, you are blessed."

Proverbs 23:26 (NLT) O my son, give me your heart. May your eyes take delight in following my ways.

Proverbs 3:5

------◆------

August 11

(Journal 7-19-2012)
    "Hear and obey. Lean your heart toward Me. Surround Me with songs of love. Let your blessing be heard on high. Let the angels worship with songs from your heart. Renew your love toward Me, and worship at My feet.
    Let light and life enfold you. Find delight in My love. Be strengthened by My might. Clothe yourself with Christ."

1 John 2:5 (NLT) But those who obey God's word truly show how completely they love him. That is how we know we are living in him.

Psalm 30:12
Isaiah 42:10

------◆------

August 12

(Journal 7-26-2012)
    "Bring Me your cares and your fears. Let Me replace them with My love and confidence. When you find your heart straying from what is good, return to Me. Bring Me your love, and cling to Mine."

Psalm 55:22 (NIV) Cast your cares on the LORD and he will sustain you; he will never let the righteous fall.

⸻ ⬥ ⸻

August 13

(Journal 8-20-2012)

I learned an important lesson a few days ago. I was about to share with someone something God had done in my life. After speaking a word or two, I heard in my mind the familiar command, "Don't go there." I stopped speaking, and immediately changed the subject. It was both abrupt and awkward. I felt stupid and frustrated, as I had so many times before. Why did it seem the Lord was constantly stopping me when I was about to share something spiritually significant with someone? I always reasoned that it must not have been the right timing, or maybe I would turn someone off from God. But this time I felt mad and confused about it. It seemed like I was about to share a good thing. This time I questioned the Lord, and asked Him if it was *really* Him saying, "Don't go there." I heard, **"I'm glad you asked. No, I will never stop you from saying something that gives glory to Me."** I was shocked. All this time I had been allowing myself to be tricked by the enemy.

The next time I heard, "Don't go there," I over-rode the command and shared anyway. I felt something I hadn't felt in quite a while; warmth flooded me from head to toe as I spoke, and I was filled with the joy that comes from witnessing. The woman I was speaking with got tears in her eyes and I knew God had touched her by what I said. This used to happen a lot, but somehow I allowed the enemy to shut me up. Never again!

I had prayed that God would put a 'watch upon my tongue and a guard at the door of my lips,' but now I know the enemy can use this to keep us silent if we are not careful. The Lord was patient in allowing me to make this mistake—waiting for me to recognize it as such.

Isaiah 43:10-12 (NIV) "You are my witnesses," declares the LORD, "and my servant whom I have chosen, so that you may know and believe me and understand that I am he. Before me no god was formed, nor will there be one after me. I, even I, am the LORD, and apart from me there is no savior. I have revealed and saved and proclaimed—I, and not some foreign god among you. You are my witnesses," declares the LORD, "that I am God."

Psalm 51:15
1 Peter 2:9

———————

August 14

(Journal 8-25-2012)
    "Clasp your hand in Mine, little one. I invite you on a journey—a journey of love. Bind your heart to Mine. In the midst of busyness, stay close. Let My love enfold you in your heart. Learn from Me. Bring Me your cares, and trust Me to care for you in the midst of all you care about. Clothe yourself with Christ. Find your fulfillment in Me. I am your joy. I am your delight. Dance with Me in your heart. Take delight in the One who loves you."

Isaiah 56:6a,7a (NIV) And foreigners *who bind themselves to the LORD* to serve him, to love the name of the LORD, and to worship him...these I will bring to my holy mountain and give them joy in my house of prayer.

Psalm 43:4 (NIV) Then I will go to the altar of God, *to God, my joy and my delight.* I will praise you with the harp, O God, my God.

Psalm 149:2-4

August 15

(Journal 8-27-2012)
"Do not delay to do the things that I have called you to. Give yourself to Me. Give your time to Me. Present yourself before Me as a living sacrifice. I will help you accomplish all that I have called you to. Simply look to Me. Trust in Me."

Isaiah 26:12 (NIV) LORD, you establish peace for us; all that we have accomplished you have done for us.

Psalm 90:17
Romans 12:1

August 16

(Journal 9/2012)
"Stand up, for your redemption is drawing near. Lift up your heads, lift up your eyes. Clothe yourselves in Christ and be prepared for that great day. Lace up your boots. Be prepared to run the race set before you. Ready yourselves for the battle, prepare your hearts for the long haul. Make ready for war. Prepare to meet the enemy on his own ground and do not give the devil a foothold on yours. Stand fast. Stand firm. Surrender to none."

Luke 21:25-28 (NIV) "There will be signs in the sun, moon and stars. On the earth, nations will be in anguish and perplexity at the roaring and tossing of the sea. Men will faint from terror, apprehensive of what is coming on the world, for the heavenly bodies will be shaken. At that time they will see the Son of Man coming in a cloud with power and great glory. When these things begin to take place, stand up and lift up your heads, because your redemption is drawing near."

Romans 13:12-14
1 Corinthians 9:24

———————

August 17

(Journal 10-6-2012)

It's thankfulness that puts a smile on the face, a lilt to the step, a joy in the heart, and blows away the mist of creeping darkness. Thankfulness dispels the uneasiness that wants to settle into a person's thoughts and attempts to take up permanent residence.

Praise be to God. Thank you, Jesus, for reminding me to give thanks for all things.

Ephesians 5:20 (NIV) ...always giving thanks to God the Father *for everything*, in the name of our Lord Jesus Christ.

Hebrews 12:28 (NIV) Therefore, since we are receiving a kingdom that cannot be shaken, let us be thankful, and so worship God acceptably with reverence and awe...

Colossians 2:7
Colossians 4:2

August 18

(Journal 10-14-2012)

"Let My hand guide you. Let My heart lead you in all things. Stay close and you will be rewarded. You will find life a joy and eternity a pleasure.

In Me is light, and no darkness. Delight to walk in the light. Determine to walk in My truth. Stand your ground against the evil one. I am your light, your life, your very great reward. Bask in My presence. Remain in My love. Be strengthened by My might, for I delight in you."

1 John 1:5-7 (NIV) This is the message we have heard from him and declare to you: God is light; in him there is no darkness at all. If we claim to have fellowship with him yet walk in the darkness, we lie and do not live by the truth. But if we walk in the light, as he is in the light, we have fellowship with one another, and the blood of Jesus, his Son, purifies us from all sin.

Ephesians 6:8
John 15:9-11

August 19

(Journal 10-16-2012)

"For all who come to Me, I offer a salvation too great to comprehend. Take from Me. It is a gift. I bestow upon you many good things, but life, abundant life, is the greatest. I will live through you. I will fill you with Myself. I will pour out My strength through you. I will lead you to a destiny filled with Me. Rejoice in the life I give you. Rejoice in My love."

Hebrews 2:3 (NIV) ...how shall we escape if we ignore such *a great salvation?* This salvation, which was first announced by the Lord, was confirmed to us by those who heard him.

Romans 6:23
Galatians 2:20

August 20

(Journal 11-14-2012)

Psalm 116:1 became a significant verse for me this week. After reading, *"I love the Lord, because He has heard my voice and my supplications. Because He has inclined His ear to me...,"* I was led to speak out loud my own reasons for loving the Lord. "I love you, Jesus, because you..." I prayed on and on, and the joy increased as I went. My love increased as well.

What a wonderful way to worship the Lord and give Him thanks and praise.

Later, I started telling John, "I love you because you..." (None of this, 'I love you just because I love you'.)

Psalm 116:1-2 (NKJV) I love the LORD, because he has heard my voice and my supplications. Because he has inclined his ear to me, therefore will I call upon him as long as I live.

1 John 4:19

August 21

(Journal 11-17-2012)

I awoke this morning with a question in my mind that I felt was from the Lord:

"Why are you acting as if you are in authority over your husband when God has placed *him* in authority over you?"

I felt it was a question for me to consider and take to heart, as well as a question for me to present to other women.

"Help me, Father, to delight in honoring my husband by submitting to his authority."

Genesis 3:16 (NLT) Then he said to the woman, "I will sharpen the pain of your pregnancy, and in pain you will give birth. *And you will desire to control your husband, but he will rule over you.*"

1 Corinthians 11:3 (NLT) But there is one thing I want you to know: The head of every man is Christ, *the head of woman is man,* and the head of Christ is God.

1 Timothy 2:11-14 (NIV) A woman should learn in quietness and full submission. I do not permit a woman to teach or to have authority over a man; she must be silent. For Adam was formed first, then Eve. And Adam was not the one deceived; it was the woman who was deceived and became a sinner. (*The fact that Adam and Eve are cited shows this verse was not just a cultural practice for that New Testament time period.*)

1 Corinthians 11:9-10 (NLT) And man was not made for woman, *but woman was made for man.* For this reason, and because the angels are watching, a woman should wear a covering on her head to show she is under authority. (*Vs. 15 says long hair is our covering.*)

Ephesians 5:22-24 (NLT) For wives, this means submit to your husbands as to the Lord. For a husband is the head of his wife as Christ is the head of the church. He is the Savior of his body, the church. As the church submits to Christ, so you wives should submit to your husbands *in everything.*

Colossians 3:18 (NLT) Wives, submit to your husbands, as is fitting for those who belong to the Lord.

1 Peter 3:5 (NLT) This is how the holy women of old made themselves beautiful. They trusted God and accepted the authority of their husbands. For instance, Sarah obeyed her husband, Abraham, and called him her master. You are her daughters when you do what is right without fear of what your husbands might do.

Titus 2:3-5 (NLT) Similarly, teach the older women to live in a way that honors God. They must not slander others or be heavy drinkers. Instead they should teach others what is good. These older women must train the younger women to love their husbands and their children, to live wisely and be pure, to work in their homes, to do good, *and to be submissive to their husbands. Then they will not bring shame on the word of God.*

Esther 1:17-18 (NIV) "For the queen's conduct will become known to all the women, and so they will despise their husbands and say, 'King Xerxes commanded Queen Vashti to be brought before him, but she would not come.' This very day the Persian and Median women of the nobility who have heard about the queen's conduct will respond to all the king's nobles in the same way. *There will be no end of disrespect and discord.*"

August 22

(Journal 11-20-2012)
"Rejoice, little one, for great is the love of your Father. I come to you as you kneel before Me. I hear your heart as you pray. I am ever before you—ever by your side, ever longing to draw you closer. Come to Me, little one. Come often and let Me fill you with joy. Let My love abide within you. Release your fears to Me—do not let the enemy hold you captive."

John 15:9-12 (NKJV) "As the Father loved me, I also have loved you; abide in my love. If you keep my commandments, you will abide in my love, just as I have kept my Father's commandments and abide in His love. These things have I spoken to you, that My joy may remain in you, and that your joy may be full. This is My commandment, that you love one another as I have loved you."

August 23

(Journal 11/2012)

"Live close to Me, little one. Stand your ground against the snares of the enemy. Cling to Me. Find in Me the strength you need. Find in Me your joy and delight. Learn to love Me more. Rest your head upon My breast. Let your thoughts be led by My Spirit."

Romans 8:5-6 (NLT) Those who are dominated by the sinful nature think about sinful things, but those who are controlled by the Holy Spirit think about things that please the Spirit.

Psalm 18:1-2

August 24

(Journal 12/2012)

"Strengthen yourself in Me. I am your strong tower. Run to Me for refuge any moment of the day. Find in Me the love and understanding you need. I am your hope and your joy, your very great reward. Find in Me the delight I long to give you. Rejoice in My love for you, rejoice."

Psalm 46:1 (NKJV) God is our refuge and strength, a very present help in trouble.

Psalm 71:5
Psalm 43:4

August 25

(Journal 12-4-2012)

"Help me, Jesus, to see your artistry in all of creation. Open my eyes to see your handiwork. I will look for and love what my beloved has done. Forgive me for all the times I didn't notice. Help me to take the time, when I have an opportunity, to look closely at what you've done."

(Journal 12-5-2012)

We think that a bouquet of flowers from a lover is delightful. God has given us a *world* of flowers. What a wonderful expression of his love.

Isaiah 45:12
Psalm 65:5-13
John 1:1-3

August 26

(Poem from the Lord, 2006) – Come Unto Me

"When tired and worn, come rest in Me,
For grace is here, and peace is free.
Come lay your head upon My breast,
For in My word I promised rest.

Just close your eyes and breathe in deep,
For I have promises to keep.
My grace and peace I give to you,
Just as I promised I would do."

August 27

(Journal 12-5-2012)

Here it is, December 5th, and I am sitting out on the back step in a jumper with a long sleeve t-shirt. It's beautiful!

The rest of the family went golfing, but I stayed home to work on Christmas cards. Now I wish that I had gone with them—cards can wait! "It's nice to write while the house is quiet"—that was my reasoning.

"Thank you, Jesus, for the cool fresh air."

"It's been a long time, little one, since you have sought My heart. Listen with your heart as well as your ears. Take in all that is before you. Delight in Me.

Bask in My love for you. Let Me minister to your heart, and bring joy to your mind."

"Thank you, again, Jesus, for this time."

2 Chronicles 14:7 (NIV) "Let us build up these towns," he said to Judah, "and put walls around them, with towers, gates and bars. The land is still ours, because we have sought the LORD our God; *we sought him and he has given us rest on every side.*" So they built and prospered.

Psalm 40:16
Psalm 21:6

August 28

(Journal 12-9-12)

"Stay close, little one, stay close. Find in Me your strength. Find in Me your all in all. I will lead and guide you as you cling to Me. I am your strong tower—your refuge. Never neglect your time with Me. You cannot live apart from Me and expect that I will meet all your needs. I am here for you, but you must come. Find joy in Me, little one. I long to fill you with joy overflowing but you have neglected your time with Me. You have closed your heart to My words.

Delight yourself in Me and I will give you the desires of your heart."

Deuteronomy 13:4 (NLT) "Serve only the LORD your God and fear him alone. Obey his commands, listen to his voice, and cling to him."

2 Samuel 22:2-3

August 29

(Journal 12-19-2012)

"In Me, is your very great reward. Stand fast till the end and you will not be disappointed. Grasp My hand tightly. I am here. Strength and love be unto you.

Learn to listen, little one. You have much to learn. I will teach you as you practice listening. You will be rewarded for your diligence. Do not give up. Delight yourself in My presence. Let your focus be on Me. Take in all that I desire to give you. Let My love enfold you. I am here. Trust Me.

Enrich your life in My presence. Establish your heart into My keeping."

Isaiah 55:3 (NLT) "Come to me with your ears wide open. Listen, and you will find life. I will make an everlasting covenant with you. I will give you all the unfailing love I promised to David."

Psalm 86:11

August 30

(Journal 12-20-2012)
"May your heart glow with the light of My love. As you delight in the sun coming in through your lace curtains, little one, may you delight in the love you sense shining in upon your heart. I love you. I delight in you.

Spend yourself on My behalf. Struggle to show yourself approved. Abide in Me. Do not let your heart grow lazy or weak. Strengthen that which remains."

Colossians 1:28-29 (NLT) So we tell others about Christ, warning everyone and teaching everyone with all the wisdom God has given us. We want to present them to God, perfect in their relationship to Christ. That's why I work and struggle so hard, depending on Christ's mighty power that works within me.

2 Timothy 2:15a (NIV) Do your best to present yourself to God as one approved...

Hebrews 6:12
Revelation 3:2

August 31

(Journal 12-29-2012)

I asked the Lord if he had a message for me. In a vision, the Lord placed a crown upon my head, and said it was a crown of joy, and that I would minister to others out of the overflow of this joy. I wondered if this was in scripture—'a crown of joy', and I sensed the Lord smiling and saying, **"Go ahead and look."**

I first looked up 'joy', in my concordance, but didn't find it in association with a crown. (I stopped looking too soon.) Then I looked up 'crown', and found the following verse: Isaiah 35:10 (NLT) "Those who have been ransomed by the Lord will return. They will enter Jerusalem singing, crowned with everlasting joy. Sorrow and mourning will disappear, and they will be filled with joy and gladness."

I saw that God does give a 'crown of joy', and my heart was satisfied.

Isaiah 51:11 (NIV) The ransomed of the LORD will return. They will enter Zion with singing; everlasting joy will crown their heads. Gladness and joy will overtake them, and sorrow and sighing will flee away.

Nehemiah 8:10

"My child,
let not the thoughts of your mind
stem from vanity.
For if such arises,
cut it asunder
before it blossoms into pride."

(Journal 7-27-1982)

"My love is unconditional.
My blessings are conditional."

(Journal 7-23-2014)

September 1

(Journal 1-5-2013)
"**Listen to the heart of your Father, for your Father is here, ready to meet your needs, ready to share with you intimate closeness. Wash away those feelings of guilt with a sense of My nearness. When the enemy would accuse you to yourself, turn your back on him. Let him see you clinging to Me, and know that his efforts are futile. Rest in My love. Cling to My life. Be strengthened, be restored.**

I love you, little one."

Joshua 23:8 (NLT) "Rather, cling tightly to the LORD your God as you have done until now."

Hebrews 10:22 (NLT) Let us go right into the presence of God with sincere hearts fully trusting him. For our guilty consciences have been sprinkled with Christ's blood to make us clean, and our bodies have been washed with pure water.

September 2

(Journal 1-9-2013)
"**I forgive you, little one. Be forgiven. Know that I love you, and that your Father is strong on your behalf.**

Trust Me to bring about what you desire. Lay your requests at My feet, then look to Me as a baby bird looks to its mother. Trust that I desire to meet your needs. Trust that I am here watching over you. I am your strength and your shield, lean on Me."

Psalm 5:3 (NIV) In the morning, O LORD, you hear my voice; in the morning I lay my requests before you and wait in expectation.

Philippians 4:6-7
Psalm 121

September 3

(Journal 1-10-2013)

"I will be with you, little one, do not fear. Stretch out your hand to Me for help. I will strengthen you. In Me is life. I long to give you life more abundant, but you must spend time in My presence to enjoy Me fully. You will minister to others out of the overflow of spending time in My presence. You will be light and life to others as you hold out My Spirit to a dying world. Bring them in. Seek and save My lost sheep. Bring My life to their darkness."

Luke 19:10 (NIV) "For the Son of Man came to seek and to save what was lost."

1 John 1:2
1 John 5:11-12

September 4

(Journal 1-12-2013)

"Be lifted up, little one. I am your strength. Delight yourself in Me. Increase your love for Me. Do not let the enemy snatch from you that which I have given you. Stand your ground. Set your heart on things above, not on things of the earth. Let your focus be on Me, and My love for you. Remember My words. **Remember the truths I have spoken to your heart. Review is key."**

Psalm 146:8 (NLT) The LORD opens the eyes of the blind. The LORD lifts up those who are weighed down. The LORD loves the godly.

Luke 10:27
2 Peter 1:12-13
Colossians 3:1-3

September 5

(Journal 1-16-2013)
"Find refreshment in Me, little one. Know the joy of My presence. In you, I delight. Respond to My love."

"Thank you for all the years, Father, that you have made me feel loved. I rejoice in you."

Acts 3:20a (NLT) "Then times of refreshment will come from the presence of the Lord..."

Psalm 21:6 (NIV) Surely you have granted him eternal blessings and made him glad with the joy of your presence.

September 6

(Journal 1-16-2013)
"Father, help me to get to bed early enough, so that I can wake up early enough. May this be a year of waking up

earlier and being more profitable as a wife, mother, prayer warrior, writer and artist. Help me to fulfill the purpose You have for me on this earth. Help me to take back enemy-held territory. Help me to walk in victory in my prayer life. Help me to find a new place of deep fellowship with You. Help me to be a clean vessel You can use. Help me to glorify You through what I do and say. Help me to be a blessing to many, listening always for the guidance of the Holy Spirit in all of my dealings with others. Help me to have more zeal for Your work, more love for Your people, more grace in my daily life, new insights and understandings, new ways of sharing what You have shared with me, new ways of blessing people. Pour forth Your life through me, Your love through me; minister through me. May Your name be glorified on this earth."

John 17:4
2 Peter 1:5-8

September 7

(Journal 1-22-2013)
   "Never begrudge the time spent with Me. Other uses of your time can be like chaff that will be burned up. But time spent with Me will never be burned up."

1 Corinthians 3:12-15 (HCSB) If anyone builds on that foundation with gold, silver, costly stones, wood, hay, or straw, each one's work will become obvious, for the day will disclose it, because it will be revealed by fire; the fire will test the quality of each one's work. If anyone's work that he has built survives, he will receive a reward. If anyone's work is burned up, it will be lost, but he will be saved; yet it will be like an escape through fire.

Colossians 4:12-13 (NIV) Epaphras, who is one of you and a servant of Christ Jesus, sends greetings. *He is always wrestling in prayer for you*, that you may stand firm in all the will of God, mature and fully assured. I vouch for him that *he is working hard for you* and for those at Laodicea and Hierapolis.

September 8

(Journal 2-2-2013)

"Do not be afraid to put the pen to the page, little one. Be willing to receive from Me and do not let fear keep you from listening. I love you. I am here.

Take no thought for tomorrow. I am here in your 'today'. Each moment you spend with Me is time well spent. Each day you kneel at My feet is a day worth having. These are moments that will last for eternity, sealed and signed by Me. Take no thought for tomorrow, take thought for today. Give Me your thoughts *now*. Look for My counsel *now*. Bask in Me right *now*. Let the glow of My presence be the light that fills you for today. Walk in this light. Live in this light. You never have to walk in darkness. Those who walk in darkness have left My light. Surrender your life to Me. Surrender your will to Me, and you will not fear the light.

Let the brightness of My love surround you. Let the glow of My countenance be your delight. Rest in Me. I love you, and long for you to spend more time in My presence.

Do not fear the coming darkness. The coming darkness is only dark for those who do not walk in My light. I have rescued you from darkness and transferred you to the kingdom of light. Claim your citizenship."

Colossians 1:9-14 (NIV) For this reason, since the day we heard about you, we have not stopped praying for you and asking God to fill you with the knowledge of his will through all spiritual wisdom and understanding. And we pray this in order that you may live a life worthy of the Lord and may please him in every way: bearing fruit in every good work, growing in the knowledge of God, being strengthened with all power according to his glorious might so that you may have great endurance and patience, and joyfully giving thanks to the Father, who has qualified you to share in the inheritance of the saints in the kingdom of light. For he has rescued us from the dominion of darkness and brought us into the kingdom of the Son he loves, in whom we have redemption, the forgiveness of sins.

Matthew 6:34
Jeremiah 13:15-16

September 9

(Journal 3-10-2013)
"Take delight in all that I bring you, little one. Rest in Me as I strengthen you with My love. I delight in you, little one, when you delight in Me.

Rest your head upon My heart. Lean on Me and find the strength you need to stand. Let My love blossom in your heart. Let its beauty enthrall you. Let it be a sweet perfume to delight your senses. Rest, little one, in My love for you. For I delight in My darling. Bathe your heart in My delight. Soak in all the essence of My love for you."

"I bask in Your beauty, O Lord. I find fulfillment in Your love. I receive Your amazing peace and calm joy. I love You."

Psalm 149:4-5 (NIV) For the LORD takes delight in his people; he crowns the humble with victory. Let his faithful people rejoice in this honor and sing for joy on their beds.

1 Corinthians 1:3
Philippians 2:1-2

September 10

(Journal 3-20-2013)
　　First day of spring!
　　I was reminded last night, and this morning, of the job that God gave me to do. In 1983, God spoke a poem to me that gave me the job of 'planting':

> **"If your tears fall like dew,**
> **Upon a dusty plain,**
> **Take heart, little one,**
> **For I will send the rain,**
> **You do the planting,**
> **And I will do the rest,**
> **For the Lord of the harvest,**
> **Makes sure the seeds are blessed."**

　　God has not called me to reap; He has called me to plant. I have been frustrated as a reaper, because for me, it's like trying to fit a round peg into a square hole. It's not my job. God *may* call me to reap at times, He said, but my job is to plant seeds.
　　In 2012, the Lord said to me:
　　"Lift up *Me* and let *Me* draw people to Myself. It is never your place to force a relationship or a decision; that is the work of the Holy Spirit...some I have called to reap, some to plant. I have not called you to reap. That is why you find that people are offended when you attempt to reap. It is not your job

with them. Share Me, lift Me up. Spread the Good News, but do not demand a response. Do not close up a heart that is softening to My word. Plant and nourish. The harvesters are ready.

Paul was not called to baptize, yet it was part of the salvation process. Not all are called to every task. Trust Me to lead you toward yours. You will find delight in doing the work that I have called *you* to do. You will find the process painful if you try to do someone else's task. There are times I may call you to reap. Be open to those times, but follow My lead. Don't force your way. Don't leave the path of peace."

First day of spring—it's time to plant!

John 4:36-38
John 12:32
Psalm 126:5

September 11

(Journal 3-21-2013)
"Rejoice, little one, in your Father's love. I am mighty to save. I will rescue you from the darkness and bring you into the light again. Relish your time with Me. In Me is sweet escape from the worries and fears of the day. In Me is peace and calm. Rest in Me. Find peace in Me. Let your labors cease in My presence.

Beautiful, beautiful are the hands of the Lord, bringing all to order. Let the presence of the Lord be your strong tower. Rest in Me. You will not stand ashamed."

Zephaniah 3:17 (NLT) For the LORD your God is living among you. He is a mighty savior. He will take delight in you with gladness. With his love, he will calm all your fears. He will rejoice over you with joyful songs.

Matthew 11:28-29
Psalm 91

━━━━━◦•⊱✦⊰•◦━━━━━

September 12

(Journal 3/2013)
    "Let My love flow through you. Receive My love for yourself and pass the excess on to others. When I shower love, I shower abundantly."

Jude 1:1-2 (NIV) Jude, a servant of Jesus Christ and a brother of James, to those who have been called, who are loved by God the Father and kept by Jesus Christ: Mercy, peace and love be yours in abundance.

Romans 5:5
John 7:37-39
John 13:34-35
1 John 4:11-12

━━━━━◦•⊱✦⊰•◦━━━━━

September 13

(Journal 4-1-2013)
    "Grow in grace, little one. Give grace to others and receive it for yourself. Rest in Me, for I am tender towards you. Grow as a flower in My garden, little one. Add beauty to the world around you. Trust Me to replenish you with the rain—the water you need to grow. Trust Me to give you the light to strengthen

your frame. Let Me pour out My love and life into you. Be energized by My Spirit."

"...Help me to communicate, Father..."

"Give of your heart to others, little one. Do not be afraid to pour My love into them."

Isaiah 58:11 (NIV) The LORD will guide you always; he will satisfy your needs in a sun-scorched land and will strengthen your frame. You will be like a well-watered garden, like a spring whose waters never fail.

John 15:1

September 14

(Journal 4-14-2013)
"Know Me, little one. Know that I love you. Long for My presence, as a lover longs for the object of his affection. So I desire for you to long for Me. Increase your love for Me, little one. Draw near; you are in need of My presence as the enemy buffets your soul. This is only round one. Prepare for the fight. Find strength in Me. I am here to establish your heart. Bask in My love. Receive it. Grow strong in My grace as I lavish My love on you."

"I receive your love, Jesus."

"Pour out your love upon others, little one. The time is short. Pour out your love while you are here."

Psalm 63:1 (NKJV) O God, You are my God; early will I seek You: my soul thirsts for You; my flesh longs for You in a dry and thirsty land where there is no water.

1 John 4:7-21

September 15

(Journal 4-30-2013)

"Let My love transform you, little one. Let it fill you with sweet savors and thrill you to the core. I am here. No need for fear. Let My love lift you up. Rejoice! Though your lungs fill with fluid—rejoice! Though your breathing is difficult—rejoice! Am I not able to be everything to you—even your healer? Am I not able, with a touch, to turn your health around? Rejoice!"

"Yes, Father, you are. You are able!"

"Grand is the design I have formed and planned for you. Your mind would not be able to wrap around it at this moment, were I to reveal it to you. So I allow you to live one day at a time—concealing from you all that is unnecessary to burden you with.

Delight in Me. This is your calling. This is your task. Delight in Me, and restrain your feet from wandering down paths I have not called you to. Stay close to Me. My plans will unfold as you are beholding Me.

My love for you is great,
My plans for you are never late.
I give My children as I deem best,
And lovingly I shoulder the rest.
Stay strong, stay true,
Just stand and watch what I will do."

Psalm 103:1-4 (NLT) Let all that I am praise the LORD; with my whole heart, I will praise his holy name. Let all that I am praise the LORD; may I never forget the good things he does for me. He forgives all my sins and heals all my diseases. He redeems me from death and crowns me with love and tender mercies.

Jeremiah 29:11

September 16

(Journal 5-22-2013)
 With a heart nearly bursting with love for the Lord after looking back in a journal, I heard:
 "Wind your heart around My love for you, little one. Weave your emotions around My care. Let My love for you become a beautiful pattern in a tapestry that we weave together. Let us share in love the joy and delight we have for one another."

1 Corinthians 8:3 (NIV) But the man who loves God is known by God.

Psalm 147:11
1 John 4:19

September 17

(Journal 5-23-2013)
 "Learn to take messages, little one. Be a good secretary for Me and I will use you to bless others and to bring joy and comfort into their lives. Encourage them, little one. This is your task. I love you."

Jeremiah 1:2 (NLT) The LORD first gave messages to Jeremiah during the thirteenth year of the reign of Josiah son of Amon, king of Judah.

1 Corinthians 14:3

September 19

(Journal 5-25-2013)
    "Grow in grace, little one. Know the ministry that I have for you will be a joy to yourself as well as others. I call you to reach out to others in love. Read what I ask you to read, little one. Learn and grow. Develop the skills and abilities that will enable you to perform the duties I have for you. Do not be afraid. I will stretch you—yes, but you will be glad for the stretching in the end. Grow in love. Grow in grace. Grow in joy as you look to Me."

2 Peter 3:18 (NIV) But grow in the grace and knowledge of our Lord and Savior Jesus Christ. To him be glory both now and forever! Amen.

Ephesians 4:16
John 15:16-17

September 20

(Journal 6-13-2013)
    "Cling to Me, little one. Rest in My love. You are not alone in your struggles. I am here, watching over

you, and protecting you, guiding you and helping you to reach your safe haven."

Psalm 121:2-4 (NIV) My help comes from the LORD, the Maker of heaven and earth. He will not let your foot slip—he who watches over you will not slumber; indeed, he who watches over Israel will neither slumber nor sleep.

Psalm 59:16-17
Psalm 32:7

September 21

(Journal 6-15-2013)
  "I open up before you, little one, the world of My presence. As you draw near to Me, you find vast treasure untapped, vast resources at your request, myriads of angels at your disposal, height and depth and breadth to get to know. The power is limitless. My presence with you is a world of wonders, a vast array of possibilities."

Ephesians 1:18-21 (NIV) I pray also that the eyes of your heart may be enlightened in order that you may know the hope to which he has called you, the riches of his glorious inheritance in the saints, and his incomparably great power for us who believe. That power is like the working of his mighty strength, which he exerted in Christ when he raised him from the dead and seated him at his right hand in the heavenly realms, far above all rule and authority, power and dominion, and every title that can be given, not only in the present age but also in the one to come.

Ephesians 3:17-19

September 22

(Journal 6-29-2013)
   "Your schedule will dictate your life unless you come and ask *Me* what to do. You will go from one thing to another until you come to Me for rest."

   Oh, the joy of coming to Jesus! I have not felt such peace in weeks. I have been forgetting to sit in the presence of Jesus and ask, "What would *You* have me do?"
   Immediately, I was filled with the joy, peace and love of His presence. All of these washed over me as He gave me, again, the picture of the waves washing over my legs in Florida—the sun warming my soul.

Hebrews 4:9-10 (NIV) There remains, then, a Sabbath-rest for the people of God; for anyone who enters God's rest also rests from his own work, just as God did from his. Let us, therefore, make every effort to enter that rest, so that no one will fall by following their example of disobedience.

Romans 14:7-8
Ephesians 2:10

September 23

(Journal 7-28-2013)
   "I delight in you, little one. Your heart is set on following Me. I will clear the way before you. Rest in Me. Find in Me your great delight. Delight in Me and I will give you the desires of your heart.

Ponder the truths of My word. Clasp My hand in yours. Let us walk together as lovers and friends. I delight in your friendship. I delight in you."

Isaiah 57:14-15 (NIV) And it will be said: "Build up, build up, prepare the road! Remove the obstacles out of the way of my people." For this is what the high and lofty One says—he who lives forever, whose name is holy: "I live in a high and holy place, but also with him who is contrite and lowly in spirit, to revive the spirit of the lowly and to revive the heart of the contrite."

Psalm 119:15
Psalm 37:4

September 24

(Journal 2013)
　　"Stay close to Me today. Wrap your heart and your arms around Me. Minister to Me through praise and worship as I minister to you through peace and joy."

Psalm 29:2 (NLT) Honor the LORD for the glory of his name. Worship the LORD in the splendor of his holiness.

1 Chronicles 16:9-10
Isaiah 55:12

September 25

(Journal 8-3-2013)
    "Draw near, little one, draw near. Let your heart be an open book before Me. Hold nothing back. Share all with Me."

    "What is in my heart, Father? I don't even know what is in my heart."

    "You don't know what's in your heart because you haven't been sharing it with Me."

Psalm 73:28 (NKJV) But it is good for me to draw near to God: I have put my trust in the Lord GOD, that I may declare all thy works.

Psalm 62:8

September 26

(Journal 8-6-2013)
    "Learn and grow, little one. I have much to teach you. Open your heart to instruction. Humble yourself before Me and your life will always be full of new discoveries. I delight to instruct My children who are open to My instruction. Learn well, and you will be used to instruct others."

Isaiah 28:26 (NIV) His God instructs him and teaches him the right way.

Psalm 25:9
Proverbs 8:33
Job 35:10-11

September 27

(Journal 8-21-2013)
"Do not fear, little one. Your Father is near. Do not wander on lonely paths when I am here to comfort. Long for Me. Seek to know Me better. Train yourself to listen. Turn to Me in time of need. I long to be everything to you. Send your love My way on wings of prayer. Accept the challenge of a life lived in My presence."

Isaiah 41:10 (NIV) "So do not fear, for I am with you; do not be dismayed, for I am your God. I will strengthen you and help you; I will uphold you with my righteous right hand."

Deuteronomy 30:20 (NIV) ...and that you may love the LORD your God, listen to his voice, and hold fast to him. For the LORD is your life, and he will give you many years in the land he swore to give to your fathers, Abraham, Isaac and Jacob.

Psalm 65:4 (NIV) Blessed are those you choose and bring near to live in your courts! We are filled with the good things of your house, of your holy temple.

September 28

(Journal 9-5-2013)
"Enter into My rest. I give you rest in My presence. I desire that all My children would learn how to enter into My rest, that place of joy and peace.

Listen to My voice often. I desire to lead you in new paths, but you must stay close, lest you lose the way. I am the way. Cling to Me.

Share My love with others. Do not keep it for yourself alone. It was meant to be shared. Yes, I'm talking about writing, for one thing..."

Romans 14:17 (NIV) For the kingdom of God is not a matter of eating and drinking, but of righteousness, peace and joy in the Holy Spirit...

Isaiah 28:11-12
Hebrews 4:8-11

September 29

(Journal 9-10-2013)
"Close your ears to falsehood. Open your heart to Me. Give no place to the enemy, who seeks to attack you in your thoughts. Resist him! Place your trust in Me. I am here.

Rejoice! Rejoice! For great is the love of your Father. Let My love fulfill you. Find joy in My presence."

2 Timothy 4:18 (NIV) The Lord will rescue me from every evil attack and will bring me safely to his heavenly kingdom. To him be glory for ever and ever. Amen.

1 Peter 5:8-9a (NIV) Be self-controlled and alert. Your enemy the devil prowls around like a roaring lion looking for someone to devour. Resist him, standing firm in the faith...

John 8:44
James 4:7

September 30

(Journal 9-14-2013)

"Trust Me, little one. Learn to trust Me more. Pour out your heart to Me. Renew your love for Me. Cling to Me. Let joy be the response of your heart toward Me, as I envelope you in My love. Cast your cares on Me, little one. I will revive you. I will lift you up above your cares, to that place where the sun shines always."

1 Peter 5:7 (NLT) Give all your worries and cares to God, for he cares about you.

Philippians 4:6-7

"The more you pray,
the easier it will be to pray.
The less you pray,
the harder it will be to pray.
Prayer is like a muscle;
it needs to be exercised
or it will diminish."

(Journal 6/2014)

"The time you spend in prayer pays off.
Never think it is wasted time."

(Journal 1-29-2012)

October 1

(Journal 10-14-2013)
"Just being in Your presence is a joy and a delight. In Your presence, the deafening sounds of the world disappear. Like one who dips beneath the surface of a lake and hears only the stillness, I immerse myself into Your quiet."

"I sense Your power pouring through every pore. I am awash in Your love."

Zephaniah 3:17 (HCSB) "Yahweh your God is among you, a warrior who saves. He will rejoice over you with gladness. He will bring you quietness with His love. He will delight in you with shouts of joy."

Psalm 46:10a (NIV) "Be still, and know that I am God;"

October 2

(Journal 10/2013)
"I sit before You, Lord, waiting expectantly for Your loving Spirit to speak to my heart. Lead me this day, Father. Instruct my heart. Help me to have a heart of obedience."

"Follow the path set out for you, little one. Lean on Me. I am your brightness—your very great reward. Clasp your hand in Mine. Sing because I love you. Sing because in Me you will find your rest. Sing because I delight in you. Sing because you delight in Me. Sing because your heart is learning to be light. Sing for joy, sing for love; sing, sing, sing. Do not let your voice be quiet, do not let your tongue be still. For the moment—sing."

Psalm 47:6 (NLT) Sing praises to God, sing praises; sing praises to our King, sing praises!

Genesis 15:1 (NIV) After this, the word of the LORD came to Abram in a vision: "Do not be afraid, Abram. I am your shield, your very great reward."

Isaiah 61:3 (NKJV) To console those who mourn in Zion, to give them beauty for ashes, the oil of joy for mourning, *the garment of praise for the spirit of heaviness;* that they might be called trees of righteousness, the planting of the LORD, that he may be glorified.

Psalm 13:6

October 3

(Journal 10-30-2013)

"Long for Me, little one—long for My presence. Lift your heart to Me. Feel My sweet peace as I encircle you. Never feel that you are alone. I am here, beside you—within you.

Stand and face the adversary. Be strong in My word and in My mighty power. Surrender your will to Mine and I will fight for you.

Glean wisdom, glean truth, glean grace to help in time of need.

Stand strong. Be on your guard. Your adversary prowls around like a roaring lion seeking someone to devour. Your safety is in My care, but you must come to Me.

Fly, little one, fly into My arms. Let My arms enfold you as you find sweet relief. Trust Me. Let your heart be abandoned into My care."

Exodus 14:14 (NIV) "The LORD will fight for you; you need only to be still."

Proverbs 23:23 (NIV) Buy the truth and do not sell it; get wisdom, discipline and understanding.

James 4:7
1 Peter 5:7-9

October 4

(Journal 11-3-2013)
      "You will learn to speak, little one. You will learn to share a word in due season. Trust Me to lead you.
      Develop an ear for others. Listen to all that is going on around you. You miss so much because your attention is on other things. Train yourself to focus on others. Listen to their heart as well as their words.
      Good job in listening to My Spirit today.
      Be led by My love."

Proverbs 15:23 (NKJV) A man has joy by the answer of his mouth, and a word spoken in due season, how good it is!

Philippians 2:3-4

October 5

(Journal 11-8-2013)
      "Listen. My voice calls out to you. Do you hear? Do you know that I am looking and longing for the

voice of My beloved? Do you desire to hear tender words? Then come to Me. Find in me all that you seek. You long to be used by Me. That will only happen as you spend time in My presence. As you listen to Me, I will instruct you. I will lead you in the way that you should go. Trust Me. Lean on Me. Don't be afraid, little one. I love you."

"Help me to go beyond where I've ever been in my relationship with You, Father. Help me to find that place of solid faith."

Psalm 27:8 (NLT) My heart has heard you say, "Come and talk with me." And my heart responds, "LORD, I am coming."

Psalm 119:77 (NLT) Surround me with your tender mercies so I may live, for your instructions are my delight.

October 6

(Journal 12-14-2013)
"Place your heart in My care, little one. I will provide safe keeping. I love you and long to nurture you when you are feeling unnurtured. When your heart is sad within you—I care. When life is not what you thought it would be—I care. When peace eludes you and comfort is rare—I care. When your heart is breaking from the weight of concern—I care. I do not leave you comfortless. Come to Me."

"I leave my care at Your feet, oh Lord. For You are everything to me. I do not need another to comfort me when I have You. I love You. You are my joy and delight, and I delight myself in You. Hope springs eternal. You have put Your love in my heart and there is joy within—joy overwhelming. Thank You."

Isaiah 51:12a (NLT) "I, yes I, am the one who comforts you."

2 Corinthians 1:3-4
Isaiah 66:13

———

October 7

(Journal 12-30-2013)

After listening to a Christian radio program about child trafficking, I began to feel ineffective. I thought, "What am I doing; only writing?" As I started to pray, I heard in my heart, **"Your place is no less important, I need men and women standing up for morality, standing up for what is right. They are the pillars in society."**

After reading this, I thought of how I check with John before writing something, to find out if it's something I should feel passionate about and take time to write about.

"I'm looking to him as the head of the home," I told the Lord. "I've been looking to John."

"No, little one, you've been looking for an excuse. You've been looking for an excuse not to write what I have put upon your heart. I have called you to be a writer—so write. He will not share the same burden I give to you. I am giving him other passions. You are to fulfill yours. If you try to involve him in your passions, yours will fizzle out. Write, when I give you the passion to write. The passion is your fuel for action. Don't waste it.

You must write, little one. You must write My heart because you hear My heart. Convey My heart to the people."

"Just as You have called John to be passionate in the pulpit, You have called me to be passionate in print."

2 Corinthians 3:12 (NIV) Therefore, since we have such a hope, we are very bold.

Acts 24:25

October 8

(Journal 1-7-2014)

"Hang close to Me, little one. Let your heart be attached to Me. Love what I love. Hate what I hate. Focus on what I lead you to focus on. Turn your gaze upon Me. Let Me lift you up above the mud and the mire." (I was given a picture of the Lord reaching down and lifting me under the arms like a father lifts a small infant.)

"Be free, little one. Be free. Set your affections on Me. Rest on My chest, little one. Draw near, draw near."

Psalm 40:2 (NIV) He lifted me out of the slimy pit, out of the mud and mire; he set my feet on a rock and gave me a firm place to stand.

John 8:36
James 4:8

October 9

(Journal 1-8-2014)

"Let the troubles of this world be your care and concern. Love those who are in need of My love. Speak My truths to them, but gently. Minister My

grace. **Prepare hearts with prayer. Bathe them in My love."**

Galatians 6:1-2 (NIV) Brothers, if someone is caught in a sin, you who are spiritual should restore him gently. But watch yourself, or you also may be tempted. Carry each other's burdens, and in this way you will fulfill the law of Christ.

2 Timothy 2:24-26

October 10

(Journal 1/2014)
Question: "What will our lives reflect as we look back on them? How did we spend our time?"

"You have spent much time with Me, little one, through the years. Your life will reflect your service to Me. You have loved Me and I have loved you. I desire for you to grow, and so I push you to spend time with Me—beyond the norm.

I call to you because I long to spend time with you, and I want you to desire Me above all else. The plans I have for you require closeness. Stay close. Stay in love. Do not let your heart grow cold. Long for Me, little one, long for Me. Let your greatest pleasure in life be to spend time in My presence. Acknowledge Me in all your ways. I will lead you and guide you as you look to Me. Let your longings be fulfilled in Me. Bask in My love for you. Stretch out your hand to Me. I implore you to come, to delight in Me."

"Praise You, Jesus, bless You, Father. Thank You for Your life in me. Thank You for Your love, Lord."

"Let My life be your great reward. Bend to My will, little one. Be faithful to follow the path I have laid out for you. When you are confused, seek My face."

Isaiah 26:7-9a (NIV) The path of the righteous is level; O upright One, you make the way of the righteous smooth. Yes, LORD, walking in the way of your laws, we wait for you; your name and renown are the desire of our hearts. My soul yearns for you in the night; in the morning my spirit longs for you.

Luke 5:16
Proverbs 3:6

October 11

(Journal 1-18-2014)
"Entreat Me, little one, on behalf of others. Let your heart overflow with love from the throne room.

Stand fast. Prepare a spread of My word for other believers to feast from. Let My word go to the inward parts to accomplish My purpose. Let My plans prevail in the hearts and lives of those around you. Bring My word to each person I lay on your heart. Be faithful as you administer My love and My life to others.

I love you, My child. Cling to Me. Find delight in Me."

Ephesians 1:15-16 (NIV) For this reason, ever since I heard about your faith in the Lord Jesus and your love for all the saints, I have not stopped giving thanks for you, remembering you in my prayers.

Philippians 1:4-6
Isaiah 55:10-11

October 12

(Journal 1-19-2014)

About a week ago, the Lord told me I was going to give a testimony at church. Today I gave this testimony:

"It may be that God wants everyone to be healed. It may be that healing is in the atonement. But it may also be that God sometimes has a requirement before someone can be healed. Just as Naaman had to dip in the Jordan seven times in order to be healed, or Paul needed to have Ananias pray for him before he could be healed, or the blind man had to go to the pool of Siloam and wash before he could receive his sight from Jesus; it may be that some need to repent of sin before they can be healed.

Many people have prayed for my foot. Even a man at our national headquarters, who had the gift of healing, prayed for my foot. I had the elders of our church pray, again, for my foot on Sunday, January 5. On Monday, alone in my room, I prayed and asked the Lord, again, to heal my foot. He said, '**No.**' Imagine that. Then He added, '**Not until I am more important to you than *walking*. Not until I am more important to you than *breathing*. Not until I am more important to you than *eating*.**'

The next day, I took time to fast and seek Him; to seek him for himself, not for healing, not for a blessing.

Two days later, I walked to the kitchen for breakfast. I felt so hungry, but these words suddenly came to mind, '**No, not until I am more important to you than walking. Not until I am more important to you than breathing. Not until I am more important to you than eating.**' I fasted again."

I also shared in my testimony how my foot was about ninety percent healed, and that I was only up at the podium because of obedience.

During the worship time, God gave me a vision of the King in His throne room, standing and holding His baby above His head as He smiled at it. Then He turned the baby toward the people to show it off as though He were proud of it. I knew the baby was me, and that the Lord was proud of me for taking a step of obedience to give my testimony, even though I was not completely healed.

I cried during the testimony. I knew I was going to, because I cried in the same spot every time I practiced. I also knew it was the Holy Spirit making me cry.

Note: It wasn't until over a year after this, that I was completely healed. One day, everything came together. I told the Lord, "I'd like to walk without pain, but if I never walk without pain again, that's up to *You*. If I die because I eat something I'm allergic to, that causes my lungs to become congested and I can't breathe, that's up to *You*. (A fear left me that day.) And, I'm going to spend time with You *before* breakfast, even though I'm really hungry." Joy filled me as the Lord said, **"I'm going to heal you today."** He led me to look up, on the internet one last time, what I was experiencing with my foot. I found something that matched my symptoms: 'Nerve Entrapment Pain.' I asked John to lay hands on my foot and pray against the nerve entrapment pain. The pain went away immediately.

I had walked with pain for over five years. It was wonderful to be able to walk without pain again.

2 Kings 5:13-14
Acts 9:10-18
John 9:6-7
James 5:14-16

October 13

(Journal 1-29-2014)
"Live in an undisturbed state. Have no fear. Reach out your hand to Me. Let love fill you to overflowing. Precious in the sight of the Lord are those who love Him.

Be a keeper of My heart, little one. Keep the treasures of My love for all to see. My love for you will encourage others.

Grow in My love. Grow stronger. Grow more faithful. Let My strength be your crowning glory. You, who are so near to My heart, rest in Me. Let My loveliness be your veil; one who is shielded from evil—hidden by My power from the evil one.

I love you, My child. Let My love bloom within your heart. Let it well up as a fountain of living water. Let the hearts of many be filled and refreshed. Give, give, give."

1 Thessalonians 3:12 (NLT) And may the Lord make your love for one another and for all people grow and overflow, just as our love for you overflows.

Psalm 31:20 (NLT) You hide them in the shelter of your presence, safe from those who conspire against them. You shelter them in your presence, far from accusing tongues.

John 15:12

October 14

(Journal 1-29-2014)

"Let love lend you mystery; mysteries to be unfolded, discovered by the hand of God. Be excited for all that I am revealing to you. Let My love render you speechless. Rest in Me, little one, loved by the Father. Blend your heart and your will with Mine.

Attached to this message is a love so great that its fulfillment will only be known at the end of the ages. You are a bearer of Good News, blessed by the Father, to be one who will share the love of God in tangible ways. Receive My messages. Receive My heart. Prepare the way for them to be received.

Let My love spring up within your heart—frothy, joyous, bubbling out the mouth, made to be shared, made to be expressed in so many ways.

Delight in Me. Delight in My love for you, for I delight in you:

> Bask in My love for you,
> Tender and sweet.
> Bask in My love,
> As you kneel at My feet.
>
> Bask in My presence,
> And share My delight.
> Know you are loved,
> By day and by night."

"Thank You, Jesus."

Psalm 92:1-2 (NLT) It is good to give thanks to the LORD, to sing praises to the Most High. It is good to proclaim your unfailing love in the morning, your faithfulness in the evening.

Psalm 36:5-10 (NLT) Your unfailing love, O LORD, is as vast as the heavens; your faithfulness reaches beyond the clouds. Your righteousness is like the mighty mountains, your justice like the ocean depths. You care for people and animals alike, O LORD. How precious is your unfailing love, O God! All humanity finds shelter in the shadow of your wings. You feed them from the abundance of your own house, letting them drink from your river of delights. For you are the fountain of life, the light by which we see. Pour out your unfailing love on those who love you; give justice to those with honest hearts.

Mark 16:15 (NLT) And then he told them, "Go into all the world and preach the Good News to everyone."

October 15

(Journal 2-3-2014)
    "Do not ignore this time with Me. Even yet, you can redeem the time. While you are still on this earth it is not too late. Come to Me. Come to Me often. Listen, learn. Repent of your lack of trust in Me. Let your heart be restored.
    May your life be enriched with My wisdom. May you be filled with understanding.
    Present your requests to Me, little one, in a spirit of trust."

Job 12:13 (NIV) " To God belong wisdom and power; counsel and understanding are his."

Proverbs 2:6
Isaiah 50:10
Philippians 4:6

October 16

(Journal 2-7-2014)
"'Repent, for the kingdom of heaven is near.' These words are your message to sinners. Take them to heart and use them as I direct you. Your life and ministry will be used by Me as I order the course of your life. Be a bold witness. Let My love pour forth from you as you seek to save those that are lost. Let My message ring from your lips, but let it pass through love.

Yes, little one, I am opening a new door of opportunity for you to witness on My behalf. Speak that which I put upon your heart."

Luke 24:47 (NIV) ...and repentance and forgiveness of sins will be preached in his name to all nations, beginning at Jerusalem.

Acts 4:29-31
2 Corinthians 3:12
Matthew 3:2
Mark 1:14-15

October 17

(Journal 2-11-2014)
"Strive to live in all that I have commanded you. Live to please Me, little one, not yourself. As you do this, you will grow beyond your highest expectations. Seek Me. Love Me. Long for Me, and you will grow in Me.

Stretch out your hand to Me, little one, I long to fill it full. Rejoice in Me. Rejoice in My love for you."

Psalm 111:10 (NLT) Fear of the Lord is the foundation of true wisdom. All who obey his commandments will grow in wisdom.

Psalm 70:4 (NIV) But may all who seek you rejoice and be glad in you; may those who love your salvation always say, "Let God be exulted!"

2 Corinthians 5:9
2 John 1:6

October 18

(Journal 2-11-2014)
"If My children would take time to spend time with Me each day they would never be lonely.
I would strengthen you with My love. Draw near."

"May my heart be renewed in You, Jesus. May my life be transformed. You are Holy. You are pure. You are good. May my life reflect Your godliness to an ungodly world."

"Be renewed day by day as you spend time with Me. Be strengthened by My love."

"I receive Your word, Father. I receive Your love."

"Live above the cares of this world. Trust Me. Peace I leave with you. My peace I give unto you. Let not your heart be troubled. Neither let it be afraid."

John 14:27 (NIV) "Peace I leave with you; my peace I give you. I do not give to you as the world gives. Do not let your hearts be troubled and do not be afraid."

———◆◆———

October 19

(Journal 2-14-2014)
    "Your joy will be full as you spend time with Me. I will fill you with insight and understanding as you look to Me to meet your needs. I know your heart. I know what you desire. But above all else, desire to be obedient to Me. Desire to honor Me. Desire to spend time in My presence. Delight in My word. Delight in My instruction. Care more for the things of God than the things of the world. Wrap yourself up in My love as you fit yourself into My plans. Let your struggle cease. I love you, little one. I am preparing good things for you. But you must fulfill your side of all that I long to accomplish through you. Do not hold back. Do not take your life into your own hands. Go with the flow of My Spirit, and I will do a mighty work in you. Rejoice!"

Psalm 119:1-2 (NLT) Joyful are people of integrity, who follow the instructions of the LORD. Joyful are those who obey his laws and search for him with all their hearts.

Psalm 119

———◆◆———

October 20

(Journal 2-15-2014)
"Do not cease to praise Me throughout your day. Praise Me as often as you can, and know that the enemy is held at bay when you praise Me."

Psalm 150

October 21

(Journal 2-23-2014)
"For many are called, but few are chosen." (Matthew 22:14)

It occurred to me this morning what 'the call' is. It's a call to repentance—few repent. I shared this with John. He agreed, and said, "It's the call from the beginning, with Cain and Abel, to the end of Revelation."

Jesus told the Pharisees, concerning John the Baptist, "You refused to believe him and repent of your sins" (Matt. 21:32). He also said, "I tell you the truth, corrupt tax collectors and prostitutes will get into the Kingdom of God before you do" (Matt. 21:31). Why will they get in? Because they repent of their sins, and turn to God.

To 'repent,' is to turn toward God's way instead of going our own way (Isaiah 53:6). 'Repent,' means 'to turn.' When we repent, we give up our own way. We no longer live for ourselves, but for God.

Acts 2:38 (NLT) Peter replied, "Each of you must repent of your sins and turn to God, and be baptized in the name of Jesus Christ for the forgiveness of your sins. Then you will receive the gift of the Holy Spirit."

A Bible study on repentance:

John the Baptist's message:
Matthew 3:1-2
Matthew 3:8
Matthew 3:11
Mark 1:4

Jesus' message:
Matthew 4:17
Mark 1:14-15

The disciples' message:
Mark 6:12

Jesus' message to his disciples after He rose again:
Luke 24:45-48

The disciples' message after Jesus returned to heaven:
Acts 2:38
Acts 3:19
Acts 20:21
Acts 26:20

God's message:
Acts 17:30

What should be our message?

October 22

(Journal 3-26-2014)

"Learn to laugh, little one, at all that would hinder your walk and bog you down. Learn to trust in

Me. You are in need of rest. You need to rest in My presence, not on your bed.

Say 'No' to the evil one who would accuse you to yourself."

"Thank You, Father. In You is sweet peace. In You is joy. In You is gladness."

Proverbs 17:22 (NIV) A cheerful heart is good medicine, but a crushed spirit dries up the bones.

Proverbs 31:25 (NLT) She is clothed with strength and dignity, and she laughs without fear of the future.

———

October 23

(Journal 3-27-2014)

"Quiet your heart, little one. Find in Me the rest you need. I give you 'true rest.' I restore you from the inside out. Wrap yourself up in Me, little one."

"I put on love, like a cozy blanket."

I felt like angels were singing to me: "Peace, peace, wonderful peace, coming down from the Father above. Wash over my spirit forever I pray, with fathomless billows of love." (Wonderful Peace by W. D. Cornell)

"Ah, little one, if you would learn the secret of being recharged every morning, then you would run on grace throughout your day."

"Immerse yourself in rivers of living water."

A verse came to mind: "Out of your heart will flow rivers of living water" (John 7:38). God gave me a vision of a river billowing toward me as I stepped into it to be immersed. I swam underwater, breathing in the Lord's presence.

Romans 13:14a (NLT) Instead, clothe yourself with the presence of the Lord Jesus Christ.

Isaiah 48:18
Psalm 23:3

October 24

(Journal 4-30-2014)
      "Learn to live in My presence, little one. Ask Me often throughout the day if I have a message for you. Then bask in the warmth, the light, the words, coming from My Spirit into yours. Sometimes I may just give you pictures. Sometimes you will understand a truth. Connect yourself to Me often, little one, just by asking."

Psalm 89:15 (NIV) Blessed are those who have learned to acclaim you, who walk in the light of your presence, O LORD.

Jeremiah 33:3 (NLT) "Ask me and I will tell you remarkable secrets you do not know about things to come."

Psalm 25:14

October 25

(Journal 6-2-2014)
"Enter into My presence, little one. I am the door. Let your heart bask in My love for you."

"Thank You, Father, for giving me the emotions of Your love. Thank You for letting me feel loved."

"My children think they know Me because they read My word. But intimacy is for those who bask in My presence—for those who commune with My heart. I love you. Let your love be given to Me through your abiding presence."

"Lord, You are my delight."

John 15:4a (NKJV) "Abide in me, and I in you."

John 15:9 (NIV) "As the Father has loved me, so have I loved you. Now remain in my love."

Psalm 140:13 (NLT) Surely righteous people are praising your name; the godly will live in your presence.

Psalm 91:1

October 26

(Journal 6-12-2014)
"You have been forgetting to come to Me for rest, little one. That is why your world feels in turmoil, why you have found no peace. Strive to be close, little one. Do not leave this time neglected. Stay tuned to My Spirit. Love, and laugh and live in Me, not apart from Me.

Hear My heart for you, little one. Listen to My heartbeat."

John 15:1-5 (NKJV) "I am the true vine; and My Father is the vinedresser. Every branch in Me that does not bear fruit He takes away, and every branch that bears fruit He prunes, that it may bear more fruit. You are already clean because of the word I have spoken to you. Abide in Me, and I in you. As the branch cannot bear fruit of itself, unless it abides in the vine, neither can you unless you abide in Me. I am the vine, you are the branches. He who abides in Me, and I in him, bears much fruit; for without Me you can do nothing."

2 Thessalonians 3:16
Matthew 11:28

October 27

(Journal 6-28-2014)
 "I love sitting outside with You, Jesus. I love the feel of summer, the sounds of summer, and the sights of summer. Thank You for giving me this pleasant Sunday afternoon."

 "Rejoice, little one. Be glad in all I bring you. Do not try to measure the past with the present, or fit the present into the future. Rejoice in this day. I have given it to you to enjoy. Delight in all that is around you. Take in the glories of summer. Enjoy the peace. Delight in the simple pleasures. Do not look for what is undone. Take a day off from your work. Relax."

Psalm 118:24 (NIV) This is the day the LORD has made; let us rejoice and be glad in it.

Ecclesiastes 5:19-20

October 28

(Journal 7-9-2014)
"Draw near, little one, draw near."

"I come to You, Father, with a heart desiring to listen. I want to be close to You. I don't want the enemy to rob me of this time. I don't want the cares of life to come between You and me. Help me, Jesus, to draw close."

"Rest in Me, child. Delight yourself in Me. Stand your ground against the evil one and do not allow him to dictate your life. Strain to hear My voice. Do all you can to take the time to listen. Be willing to weary yourself for Me. In this is rest. Find Me. Find rest."

Psalm 85:8 (NIV) I will listen to what God the LORD will say; he promises peace to his people, his saints—but let them not turn to folly.

Isaiah 43:22 (NIV) "Yet you have not called upon me, O Jacob, you have not wearied yourselves for me, O Israel."

Ephesians 6:13

October 29

(Journal 7-10-2014)
(Morning) **"Restore. Let your heart be restored to Me. Let love and faithfulness never leave you. Bind them upon your heart.**

May your heart be a heart of compassion as you seek to find and save that which is lost. Hold out My love to a dying world. Hold out My compassion. Train your heart to love—to serve. Listen to the voice of your Father. Listen and be made 'new' in your spirit. Return to Me, little one, the Shepherd of your soul. I will restore you to a heart of compassion. I will put *My* love in your heart.

Your life will be changed as you spend time with Me. Your heart will grow in love for others. I will be to you a father and a friend, encouraging, coaching, training, loving."

"Thank You, Father. Please forgive me for straying, in my heart, from Your loving presence."

The song, 'May the Mind of Christ My Savior,' comes to mind.

"Forgive me for losing so great a friendship because of doubt and fear. I am so sorry."

"I forgive you, little one."

The momentum for any revival is found in our relationship with Jesus. The will and the strength to sustain come only from His power.

(Noon) **"Fill your life with thoughts of Me. Direct your thoughts to Me. Let Me establish your heart in My care. Let boldness characterize your life. As you live in Me, My thoughts will live in you and I will accomplish My purposes in you. Let your heart be filled with the joy of My presence. Clothe yourself in Me. Listen, take time to listen. Take time to wrap yourself in My love."**

The words of the hymn, 'May the Mind of Christ My Savior,' were brought to my mind again by the Lord.

Proverbs 3:3 (NIV) Let love and faithfulness never leave you; bind them around your neck, write them on the tablet of your heart.

Luke 19:10
Matthew 9:36-38

<hr>

October 30

(Journal 7-11-2014)
    "Feel and know that I am with you." (Wave after wave of His sweet presence is passing through me.)

    "Thank You, Jesus."

    "Know that I love you. Rejoice in Me, little one, not because you feel Me, but because I love you. Be glad in heart. Let your heart be prepared to pass on this love, a love so real, so eternal—a love undying, rich and kind.
    I will quiet you with My love." (This was written through tears.)

    "Thank You, Jesus. I love You."

    "Rest in Me. Rest in My love for you."

(Today is a day of prayer and fasting.)

    "Thank You for letting me feel You again, Father."

    (This morning I felt a little of the weight of His presence as I prayed with John.)

Zephaniah 3:17 (NKJV) "The LORD your God in your midst, the Mighty One will save; he will rejoice over you with gladness; he will quiet you with his love; he will rejoice over you with singing."

1 Thessalonians 4:9-10
1 Timothy 1:14

October 31

(Journal 7-30-2014)
"Daughter, learn to pray with a heart and perspective from Me. Get to know My will by asking Me how I feel about a person or situation. Learn to pray from My perspective."

"Oh Jesus, teach me how to do this."

"Think of a person. Now ask Me how I feel about _____."

Luke 11:1
Hebrews 13:20-21

"My child,
If the road is rough and the way is long,
Open your heart and I'll give you a song.
If you see only sorrow mile after mile,
Lift up your face and I'll give you a smile."

(9-16-1983)

Beside the Sea

"Come walk with Me," I heard Him say,
He took my hand and led the way,
Along the beach, beside the sea,
In mind, my Savior walked with me.

So often I Have met Him there,
And felt Him take away my care,
Along the beach, beside the sea,
A pond, I call my 'Galilee'.

(2004)

November 1

(Journal 7-12-2014)
    "Reach out to Me, little one. Reach out your hand to receive from Me. Learn and grow. Be glad in all I bring you. Never let your heart be discouraged because things are not the way you think they should be. Rejoice in the many opportunities you have to trust in Me."

    (Evening) "Oh, Father, forgive me for my many sins. As I look back through this book I see what I have left undone. Oh, Lord, do not hold my guilt against me. I want to walk with You hand in hand as an obedient child who pleases You."

    "Oh, that you might rest in Me. Walk in My rest. Live in My rest. Know My perfect rest."

    I am reminded of a song: "Would you be free from your burden of sin? There's power in the blood..."

Psalm 19:12-13 (NLT) How can I know all the sins lurking in my heart? Cleanse me from these hidden faults. Keep your servant from deliberate sins! Don't let them control me. Then I will be free of guilt and innocent of great sin.

1 Peter 2:6 (NIV) For in Scripture it says: "See, I lay a stone in Zion, a chosen and precious cornerstone, and the one who trusts in him will never be put to shame."

———————

November 2

(Journal 7-13-2014)
    "Wait, I say, on the Lord, and He will give you the desires of your heart.

Let Me minister to you in ways that you have yet to understand. Open your heart to Me often. Come before Me with a ready mind to receive My wisdom and understanding. Clasp your hand in Mine and walk with Me. Don't think that this relationship ends when you close your book. Walk with Me throughout the day. Delight in Me. Trust Me. Let love and laughter flow from your heart to Mine. Receive My love. Grow in grace. Minister to others with the love you have received from Me. Be a joy to those who know you."

(Evening) As I was drifting off to sleep in my arm chair I heard in my spirit: **"I will be exalted in the nations. I will be exalted in the earth. Let the nations know what a great and awesome God they have."** The Lord gave me a vision of the nations learning what an awesome God they have through signs, wonders, miracles and healings. "Thank you, Jesus. Help us to make Your name known."

1 Chronicles 16
Mark 16:15-18

November 3

(Journal 7-14-2014)
"In Me is true joy. Rejoice in My presence, little one. Though the world around you is bitter, and hearts are cold, rejoice. Don't let your heart reflect the world's. You are to be set apart. You are My light in a dark world. Be glad for the opportunity to shine. Extend My mercy to a needy world. Extend My grace. Let them know there is another way. The way of peace, the way of love; a way they have not known because they have chosen to go their own way. All who follow My way will live in peace. The world

cannot follow along My way. It is the way of holiness. I am the way. Speak My truths, little one. Speak My love. Let the dying world know there is another way. Let your heart bleed with compassion. Do not condemn the world, but draw them to Me. They stand condemned already. Let them know My love imploring through you. Be My life to them. Let them see a life that is truly life. You shall capture them with love. Do not lose My fish, little one. Learn to fish well."

"Help me to be a good fisherwoman. I don't want to lose Your fish. I don't want to lose those You died for. I grew up on a fishing resort. I learned how to catch fish. Teach me to catch *Yours.*"

"...With understanding, mercy and love."

John 3:16-21 (NIV) "For God so loved the world that he gave his one and only Son, that whoever believes in him shall not perish but have eternal life. For God did not send his Son into the world to condemn the world, but to save the world through him. Whoever believes in him is not condemned, but whoever does not believe stands condemned already because he has not believed in the name of God's one and only Son. This is the verdict: Light has come into the world, but men loved darkness instead of light because their deeds were evil. Everyone who does evil hates the light, and will not come into the light for fear that his deeds will be exposed. But whoever lives by the truth comes into the light, so that it may be seen plainly that what he has done has been done through God."

Isaiah 35:8 (NIV) "And a highway will be there; it will be called the Way of Holiness. The unclean will not journey on it; it will be for those who walk on that Way; wicked fools will not go about on it."

Romans 10:14-15

November 4

(Journal 2013)

"My people are lost, little one. They need to be found. Many of them are wandering around like sheep without a shepherd. They are confused and lack understanding. They need guidance. They need to have their hearts drawn back to what is good and right and true. They need to be established—rooted and grounded in Me. But they have lost the way. They need to be found. They need to have a basis of understanding in My word. Find them, little one. I give you the task of finding them. Seek and save that which is lost. Restore to Me My precious lambs. Turn the hearts of My children back to Me, back to truth, back to godliness, back to love of purity, back to life instead of death. My people are perishing for lack of knowledge."

Jeremiah 50:6 (NIV) "My people have been lost sheep; their shepherds have led them astray and caused them to roam on the mountains. They wandered over mountain and hill and forgot their own resting place."

1 Peter 2:24-25
2 Corinthians 5:11, 18-20
Hosea 4:6a

November 5

(Journal 7-16-2014)
"Unwrap the gift that I have for you, little one— a gift so precious that it is reserved for My special ones. Do not be afraid to write. Do not be afraid to receive the gift I have for you. Yes, it is the gift of suffering. Do not try to take in all that this means. You cannot comprehend it now. Receive from My hand, and in the end you will be glad for all that I bring you."

1 Peter 2:21-23 (NLT) For God called you to do good, even if it means suffering, just as Christ suffered for you. He is your example, and you must follow in his steps. He never sinned, nor ever deceived anyone. He did not retaliate when he was insulted, nor threaten revenge when he suffered. He left his case in the hands of God, who always judges fairly.

2 Timothy 4:5 (NLT) But you should keep a clear mind in every situation. Don't be afraid of suffering for the Lord. Work at telling others the Good News, and fully carry out the ministry God has given you.

Revelation 2:3 (NLT) "You have patiently suffered for me without quitting."

A Bible study on suffering:
1 Peter 4:1-2
Hebrews 10:32-34
Hebrews 5:8
Hebrews 2:10
2 Timothy 3:12
2 Timothy 2:3
2 Timothy 1:8
2 Thessalonians 1:4-5
Colossians 1:24
Philippians 1:29
2 Corinthians 1:4-7

November 6

(Journal 7-16-2014)

"Wounds in a heart can fester and grow. It is better to deal with a wound than to cover it and ignore it."

"Father, how do You want me to deal with this wound?"

"Let Me clean it out, little one. Give it to Me to heal."

I went through a spiritual and physical action of handing over my emotional hurt.

"Thank You, Jesus, for dealing with this wound. I trust You to take care of this situation."

Sample prayer: "Lord, I was hurt by what _____ said (did). I give You this hurt, and I ask You to heal this wound." (Picture handing over your hurt to the Lord and leaving it with Him. Trust Him to work in your heart.) Then say, "I forgive _____, as You have forgiven me. Please bless _____." (He will wash away the pain.)

Isaiah 53:4-5 (HCSB) Yet He Himself bore our sicknesses, and He carried our pains; but we in turn regarded Him stricken, struck down by God, and afflicted. But He was pierced because of our transgression, crushed because of our iniquities; punishment for our peace was on Him, and we are healed by His wounds.

Psalm 147:3

November 7

(Journal 7-23-2014)

"**Child, be brave. Do the work that I have called you to do and be prepared for suffering. If I ask you to give a message to someone it is for a reason. Your work is to comply, and to deliver the message. Leave the results in My hands. Do not let trembling seize you. Fear has kept many of My children from delivering messages that were meant to encourage, train and rebuke. I would use you often if you were willing, but first you need to deliver the messages I have already given you. Do not fear, little one. I am with you.**"

(I have been asked to deliver a message that will be hard to deliver and the results could be far reaching. May the Lord soften her heart.)

Jeremiah 1:7-9 (NLT) The LORD replied, "Don't say, 'I'm too young,' for you must go wherever I send you and say whatever I tell you. And don't be afraid of the people, for I will be with you and will protect you. I, the LORD, have spoken!" Then the LORD reached out and touched my mouth and said, "Look, I have put my words in your mouth!"

2 Timothy 4:2
Titus 2:15

November 8

(Journal 8-16-2014)
"You will notice that My messages grow more and more intimate the more time you spend with Me. Do not lose those beautiful messages because of lack of time with Me."

"Lord, You know my days have been busy."

"You have a few minutes here and a few minutes there, little one. That's all you need."

"You're right. I could have taken a few minutes to ask You if You had a message for me."
After writing this, and asking the Lord if He had a message for me, I fell asleep. When I awoke, He said, **"You rested in Me, little one."**

James 4:2b (NKJV) ...Yet you do not have because you do not ask.

Isaiah 30:18

November 9

(Journal 8-17-2014)
"Rejoice, little one, rejoice. Let your joy be full as you travel this journey with Me. Never lose sight of the goal, the prize; Me—your great reward, life in Christ. I offer life eternal. Take My hand. Trust Me on this journey. Do not look back. Do not lose hope."

Matthew 5:12a (NIV) "Rejoice and be glad, because great is your reward in heaven..."

Genesis 15:1 (NIV) After this, the word of the LORD came to Abram in a vision: "Do not be afraid, Abram. I am your shield, your very great reward."

1 Peter 1:8-9 (HCSB) You love Him, though you have not seen Him. And though not seeing Him now, you believe in Him and rejoice with inexpressible and glorious joy, because you are receiving the goal of your faith, the salvation of your souls.

Philippians 3:7-14

November 10

(Journal 8-20-2014)
    "Ah, little one, you can *always* be close. Keep a thankful heart. Keep My word in your heart. Keep a song in your heart."

(Journal 9-2-14)
    "Do you see My smile, little one? You have aroused it with your thoughts of thankfulness. I hear your heart and I am delighted that you hear Mine."

    "I delight to rest in Your presence, Father. Thank You for Your peace."

Psalm 67:1 (NLT) May God be merciful and bless us. May his face smile with favor on us.

Ephesians 5:15-20

November 11

(Journal 8-29-2014)

"**Delight yourself in Me, little one, for I delight in you.**

I see your heart straining to reach Mine. I see you longing to be filled with Me, and Me alone. I hear your heart beat so close to Mine. Follow close, little one. Find your delight in Me.

Rescue the perishing. Search for the dying. Love for these will set you free from self."

The Lord brought a hymn to mind:

Channels only, blessed Master,
But with all thy wondrous power,
Flowing through us, thou canst use us
Every day and every hour.

How I praise thee, precious Savior,
That Thy love laid hold of me;
Thou hast saved and cleansed and filled me
That I might Thy channel be.

Emptied that Thou shouldest fill me,
A clean vessel in Thy hand;
With no power but as Thou givest
Graciously with each command.

Witnessing Thy power to save me,
Setting free from self and sin,
Thou who boughtest to possess me,
In Thy fullness, Lord, come in.

Jesus, fill now with Thy Spirit,
Hearts that full surrender know;
That the streams of living water
From our inner man may flow.

(The hymn entitled *'Channels Only'* was written by Mary E. Maxwell. It is now public domain.)

Isaiah 61

November 12

(Journal 9-16-2014)

What an amazing difference...to obtain something of value in the world, you work for it. To obtain something of value in the kingdom, you rest for it. Jesus wants to give us so much, but He calls us to spend time in His presence in order to receive it. He wants to give us peace, strength and joy, but He gives these things through rest.

"Come unto Me, all ye who are weary and burdened, and I will give you rest" (Matt. 11:28). It is through resting in Him that He remedies our weariness and eases our burdens, and takes up our cares. Oh, what a lovely Savior we have.

Isaiah 30:15 (NIV) This is what the Sovereign LORD, the Holy One of Israel, says: "In repentance and rest is your salvation, in quietness and trust is your strength, but you would have none of it."

Isaiah 28:12 (NLT) God has told his people, "Here is a place of rest; let the weary rest here. This is a place of quiet rest." But they would not listen.

Hebrews 4:3

November 13

(Journal 10-7-2014)

"For those that trust, is the intimacy of My fellowship. Those who doubt are lost in the waves of confusion. Cling to Me. Do not lose that place of communion with Me out of fear. Take control over the spirit of fear and rebuke it. Tell it that it has no place in you. Be strong. Be brave. Listen to My voice with a pen in hand. Listen to My voice in the middle of the night when no pen is at hand. But listen. Share your heart as well, and listen to Mine. Know that I have such a great love for you. A love that sets you free to be the person I have called you to be; one without fear, one with courage, one with great love for a lost and dying world.

Draw from Me, little one, all that you need to complete the mission and the plans I have for you. Ah, My child, dream your dreams. Let them fall under submission to Me. But use your God-given creativity to accomplish My will. Let Me pour out My life through you. Bask in Me. Draw life from My presence. Let My plans unfold as you dwell in Me. I love you. I minister to those who put their hope and trust in Me."

"Thank You, Father. I trust You."

2 Timothy 1:7 (NLT) For God has not given us a spirit of fear and timidity, but of power, love, and self-discipline.

James 1:6-7
2 Peter 1:3

November 14

(Journal 10-26-2014)
"Open your heart to Me, little one. Restore your interest in bringing healing to My people. I have called you to this. Never again let apathy stand in your path. Rebuke it in the name of Jesus. I have called you to bring healing. I have called you to restore hearts to Me. Live to serve. Live to love. Care for the lost humanity that cries out for something worthwhile; for someone to care. Show them a caring God. Show them a heart of compassion. Show them a love so great that it heals both the body and the soul when it is received.

I love you, My child. For this purpose I have raised you up. Bring all to Me, little one, your cares, your fears, your loves, and lay them at My feet. Let Me work My wonders in all. Do not cease to do the work I have called you to, out of fear. Do not be afraid, I will lead you."

Isaiah 51:7 (HCSB) "Listen to Me, you who know righteousness, the people in whose heart is My instruction: do not fear disgrace by men, and do not be shattered by their taunts."

Isaiah 57:14-20
Luke 9:6
Psalm 103

November 15

(Journal 11-17-2014)
Yesterday, during worship, an amazing, awful thing happened. God gave me a vision of Jesus Christ after his death

on the cross. I saw him in the depths of hell, with the hordes of demons in glee, while those suffering in the flames were in shock that the God of the universe was there among them. The Lord gave me the verse, "Cursed is everyone who hangs on a tree" (Galatians 3:20, NKJV). Then I knew what Jesus had done for us. He took our punishment– the pain and suffering we deserved, and I wept. I was overcome by emotion at the thought of our wonderful God suffering for us.

Then suddenly, He was lifted out from the torture and the flames, in this vision. The hordes were astonished and the people were amazed, for the grave never gives up its hold. Then Jesus preached to those still in the flames, and some believed in him. In the vision, I did not see the end result.

I shared this vision with a small group after church. I wept as I spoke, suddenly overcome with emotion again.

I asked the Lord for scriptures, for I had never considered that Jesus actually suffered the torment of hell for us. The Lord gave me these verses: "...For he was cut off from the land of the living; for the transgression of my people he was stricken. *He was assigned a grave with the wicked, and with the rich in his death,* though he had done no violence, nor was any deceit in his mouth. Yet it was the LORD's will to crush him and cause him to suffer..." (Isaiah 53:8-10, NIV).

Then I found these verses:

"But we see Jesus, who was made a little lower than the angels, now crowned with glory and honor *because he suffered death,* so that by the grace of God he might *taste death for everyone*" (Hebrews 2:9, NIV).

"But God raised him from the dead, *freeing him from the agony of death, because it was impossible for death to keep its hold on Him*" (Acts 2:24, NIV).

"For we know that since Christ was raised from the dead, he cannot die again; *death no longer has mastery over him*" (Romans 6:9, NIV).

"I tell you the truth, a time is coming and has now come when *the dead will hear the voice of the Son of God* and *those who hear will live*" (John 5:25, NIV).

"For Christ died for sins once for all, the righteous for the unrighteous, to bring you to God. He was put to death in the body but made alive by the Spirit, *through whom also he went and preached to the spirits in prison* who disobeyed long ago when God waited patiently in the days of Noah while the ark was being built" (1 Peter 3:18-20, NIV).

It wasn't just the physical death of dying that Jesus 'tasted' for us—*all* of us go through *that*. Many people go through torturous deaths. It was *hell* that he tasted for us.

I had been praying, lately, that Jesus would help me to better understand what he did for us on the cross. I didn't feel emotions for what he did, and I wanted to be able to *feel*. I wept when I first heard of what he had done for us on the cross, and periodically since, but I was ashamed of my lack of response to His great sacrifice. This recent realization has moved me to passion and renewed My love and appreciation for the Lord, regarding what he has done for us. He took my punishment so I will never have to taste death. I love Him.

November 16

(Journal 2-21-2015)
"Ah, little one, great is the love of the Lord toward you. I am mighty in power, but I seek to let My mighty power work through you. Allow Me to release My gifts through you, to bless many. Do not be afraid, for fear will only hinder My work. Be brave. Be bold. Rejoice to please Me. Rejoice to do the work that I have called you to. Be glad in all I bring you. Trust Me to fulfill My purpose in you.

Be instructed by My Spirit. Be delivered by My love. I will coach you. Stand your ground against the evil one. He seeks to destroy. I seek to employ. Brace yourself."

John 14:12 (NIV) "I tell you the truth, anyone who has faith in me will do what I have been doing. He will do even greater things than these, because I am going to the Father."

1 Corinthians 16:13-14
Philippians 1:6

November 17

(Journal 6-27-2015)

"Listen to the voice of your Father. Listen often and find in Me the source of all you need: comfort, encouragement, love, joy, peace, patience, understanding and much more.

Let My love enfold you as you rest in My presence—so great a love for one so loved. Bask in My delight. Draw near to the one who seeks to hold your hand through all difficulties.

Live as a child of God. Live to tell all of the love you have for Me. Live to be a blessing. Live to make My name known on the earth. Live to confront the wicked on their own turf. Live to push back the darkness. Live to love. Live to set the prisoners free. Be strong and courageous, and you will live."

Isaiah 12

November 18

(Journal 7-17-2015)

"In Me is sweet peace, little one. In Me is joy.

Bask in Me, for I delight in you. Find in Me your strength. When life is crowding in on you, find your comfort in Me. Slip out from the pressures and rest in My presence. There, you will find new strength to face the day. Come to Me often. Don't wait for a set time. Steal away to the quiet—find that quiet moment to rest your soul before Me. Do you think it robbery to steal time to be with Me? Am I not the Creator of time? Do not the minutes belong to Me? Is not everything in My hand? Why then should you feel that you are robbing someone or something of precious time? Am I not able to help you get more done when you spend time with Me? Am I not able to order the course of events to allow you the time you need? Things will fall into place. Trust Me."

"Please forgive Me, Jesus, for neglecting this time with You, when You have instructed me to come often. I *love* this time with You. It is the delight of my day. Yet I allow outside forces to hinder my coming. I let my lack of discipline hinder my way."

"Come often, little one, come often."

(Afternoon) "Come with a heart expectant to receive. With a heart overflowing with love, do I minister to you. Receive My joy. Receive My peace. I long to give you so much."

"I receive from You—that my heart might be overflowing to give to others. Thank You, Father. Thank You for Your precious love."

"I love You."

"I love you too, little one. (Smile, from the Lord) I have many blessings in store for you."

Psalm 23

November 19

(Journal 7-22-2015)
"Let My love revive your heart. Grow in My presence like a beautiful flower unfolding before the sun. So shall you unfold and become glorious in My sight. All that I have poured into you shall come back to reflect My glory. As you find yourself full of Me, you will delight more and more in all I bring you. I delight to pour Myself into you. You are a reflection of My glory to the world, just as the sky is a reflection of My glory, or the beauty of My creation in nature is a reflection of My glory. So I have created you to be a reflection of My glory. Never take on My glory as your own. It is not even borrowed glory. The glory is Mine and Mine alone."

Romans 8:30 (NLT) And having chosen them, he called them to come to him. And having called them, he gave them right standing with himself. And having given them right standing, he gave them his glory.

2 Corinthians 3:18
Isaiah 61:3

November 20

(Journal 8-12-2015)
"Do not weep, little one, and do not grow weary. Your Father is here—a strong tower, a place of refuge and safety. Find in Me your strength. Find in Me your life. Rejoice in My presence. Know that you are loved, and that I am for you. 'If God is for us, who can be against us?' (*Romans 8:31*).

You see, little one, you have nothing to fear. The God of the universe is on your side. Rest on that. Rest in Me. Let Me comfort you with My love, as I train your hands for war. 'We wrestle not against flesh and blood'" (*Ephesians 6:12*).

Psalm 118:6 (NIV) The LORD is with me; I will not be afraid. What can man do to me?

Psalm 56:3-4
Psalm 144:1-2

November 21

(Journal 9-9-2015)

I wrote in my prayer log: "Pray for miracles." Then I wrote, "Why have I seldom prayed for miracles before! Why do I think it seems extravagant to ask God for a miracle, as though we are asking too much, or don't deserve it. We have not because we ask not! Is anything too hard for the Lord? If He gives out the gift of miracles (1 Corinthians 12:28), then God wants miracles to be happening in every church."

"Father, forgive us for our lack of faith."

I read in Psalm 66 this morning: *"Shout joyful praises to God, all the earth! Sing about the glory of his name! Tell the world how glorious he is. Say to God, 'How awesome are your deeds! Your enemies cringe before your mighty power. Everything on earth will worship you; they will sing your praises, shouting your name in glorious songs.' Come and see what our God has done. What awesome miracles he performs for people!"* (*Psalm 66:1-5 NLT*).

Miracles bring glory to God! He wants us to trust Him for miracles! *Then* we will praise Him and shout for joy. Would we withhold this honor and praise from Him because we don't take the time or have the faith to pray for miracles?

May God be praised in our church! May we say, "Come and see what our God has done!"

Luke 18:8
John 14:12-14

November 22

(Journal 9-30-2015)
 "Stand tall in the face of adversity, little one. Minister to others with boldness. Cling to My love, cling to My truths. My righteous ones shall be bold as lions. Do not let the enemy hinder you. Let nothing turn you from your course. Minister in the love of God. Stretch out your hand to heal. Stand your ground against the enemy's attacks; so shall you win the war and gain great victory. Let Me deliver you from evil. Look to My sustaining grace.
 Listen, little one, listen to the voice of your Father. Dwell in peace. Dwell in love. Be cleansed. Be washed in the blood of the lamb. Be made new."

Proverbs 28:1 (NIV) The wicked man flees though no one pursues, but the righteous are as bold as a lion.

Isaiah 50:7 (NLT) Because the Sovereign LORD helps me, I will not be disgraced. Therefore, I have set my face like a stone, determined to do his will. And I know that I will not be put to shame.

November 23

(Journal 10-12-2015)
When life starts to feel overwhelming, it is because we are not spending time with the Lord. He gives us supernatural ability to live our lives. If we have been living in that supernatural ability, but we stop spending as much time connecting with our Savior, then we start falling back into living our lives in our own strength—in the flesh, instead of in the Spirit. We can't keep up with the supernatural pace, we are no longer 'walking in the Spirit,' and we are left in the dust. Life becomes a confusing mess until we cry out to God for help. Then we watch as He pauses, letting us get back in step with Him again.

Apart from Him we can do nothing. Apart from Him, life is a mess.

Galatians 5:25 (NIV) Since we live by the Spirit, let us keep in step with the Spirit.

John 15:5

November 24

(Journal 10-28-2015)
"Clasp My hand to your heart. Establish your friendship with Me and seek to follow Me in all things. You have known and loved Me. I have known and loved you. Repent of that which hinders our close walk together. Reveal your heart to Me. Seek to do My will. Put your hand in Mine and walk with Me. Would you cling to worthless things, little one? Would you destroy so great a friendship with a pursuit for worldly wealth, worldly pleasure? Would you desire the things that separate Me from you? Would you desire to follow a path that I have not called you to?

Yes, you have not seen the fruit of these things in your life, but a seed has been planted. I tell you these things now, so that you might uproot these desires before they blossom into pride. Take care, little one, that your pursuit is for Me, and not for worldly things."

"Oh, Father, I did not know that a seed had been planted for worldly things. Show me where this futile thing lies. Show me where I am veering off from the path that You have called me to."

"You desire worldly honor. You are not willing to write the things that I have called you to write because you are afraid of losing the esteem of the world. Give it up, little one. Be willing to give up everything for Me. Be willing to give up your reputation. Be willing to be hated for My sake."

"Please forgive me, Father. Help me to follow You wholeheartedly. Cleanse my heart, Father. Wash away my sin. Help me to have a close-knit relationship with You."

Matthew 10:22 (NIV) "All men will hate you because of me, but he who stands firm to the end will be saved."

James 4:3-4
John 12:42-43
1 Thessalonians 2:6

November 25

(Journal 10-30-2015)
"When you notice a fire, little one, do not put it out. Use the energy it produces to do the work I have called you to do. Write! Write with all your heart.

Your work is to bless, to encourage, to train and rebuke through the written word. I will empower your tongue and your pen, but don't stop writing. You have gone days without writing. Listen to the Spirit within you. I will direct your words."

Psalm 45:1 (NIV) My heart is stirred by a noble theme as I recite my verses for the king; my tongue is the pen of a skillful writer.

Jeremiah 20:8-9
Psalm 39:2-3
Luke 24:32

November 26

(Journal 11-9-2015)
    "Listen. Listen to the voice of your Father. Forever do I speak; forever do I share with those who have ears to hear. Open yours, little one. Open your heart to hear My voice.
    In Me is true joy. In Me is true peace. As you rest in My presence I bathe you with My love. Lasting peace belongs to those who rest in Me. Lasting joy is for the upright in heart.
    Enter into My rest, little one. Enter into My joy. These I reserve for those who take time to be with Me. Rejoice, for great is the love of your Father.
    Linger in the love of your Lord.
    'Peace, peace, God's peace, coming down from the Father above. Sweep over my spirit forever I pray, in fathomless billows of love.'" (Wonderful Peace, by W.D. Cornell)

Psalm 32:11 (NIV) Rejoice in the LORD and be glad, you righteous; sing, all you who are upright in heart!

Psalm 36:10
Psalm 97:11

November 27

(Journal 11-10-2015)
"Into the fullness of My Spirit there comes a song; a song for My servants to sing—a song of peace, a song of joy, a song of lasting light, a song of eternity. Breathe in My Spirit, that this song might be part of your being. Breathe in My life, breathe in My love; sense My Spirit throbbing through your body.

For those that fear My Spirit and My presence, they miss the fullness of all I long to bring them. They do not realize that it is My Spirit that brings them life—life more abundant. They are content with words on a page, but they miss the Spirit that brings these words to life. Grasp these truths, little one, that your life might be filled with the Spirit."

John 5:39 (NLT) "You search the Scriptures because you think they give you eternal life. But the Scriptures point to me!"

2 Corinthians 3:17 (NIV) Now the Lord is the Spirit, and where the Spirit of the Lord is, there is freedom.

Psalm 40:3

November 28

(Journal 11-11-2015)

"Listen to the voice of your Father. Pay close attention to My heart. I love you. Bring your thoughts before Me; your cares, your concerns. Know that it is My desire to release unto you the keys of the kingdom. I desire for you to reign and rule with Me. Set your heart on things above. Desire Me above all else.

Wash your garments, little one, that they may be white and spotless before Me. Clothe yourself in Christ. Stand before Me as a pure spotless bride; cleansed, healed, ready to do My will."

Psalm 142:2 (NLT) I pour out my complaints before him and tell him all my troubles.

Daniel 12:10 (NIV) Many will be purified, made spotless and refined, but the wicked will continue to be wicked. None of the wicked will understand, but those who are wise will understand.

2 Peter 3:14
Romans 13:14

November 29

(Journal 11-12-2015)

"Hide your life in Me, little one.
Live to please Me more and more.
Live above the shallow lives of the world.
Set your mind on things above.
I am pleased with your progress.

Live to please Me more and more.
Stand firm when the enemy attacks.
Find your strength in Me.
Abandon yourself into My care.
Trust Me to bring about your victory.
Be cleansed from all that would drag you down
      to the earth.
Let your tethers be cut.
Live to please Me more and more."

Colossians 1:10-12 (NIV) And we pray this in order that you may live a life worthy of the Lord and may please him in every way: bearing fruit in every good work, growing in the knowledge of God, being strengthened with all power according to his glorious might so that you may have great endurance and patience, and joyfully giving thanks to the Father, who has qualified you to share in the inheritance of the saints in the kingdom of light.

1 Thessalonians 2:12
Revelation 3:4
2 Corinthians 5:9-10

November 30

(Journal 11-14-2015)
      Yesterday morning the Lord gave me a message when I asked Him if He had a message for me. It was a beautiful message.
      Later, while looking up verses for *Her Secret Garden*, I read a message from the Lord in my journal on *June 2012*. In the message the Lord told me, **"Listen, little one, and I will always share My heart with you because I love you. I have a message for you in your deepest, darkest moments, and I have a message for you in your brightest moments..."** I wanted to hear from the Lord

again, and so I asked Him if He had a message for me. (Silence) I asked again. (Silence) The silence was disturbing, especially after I had just read of Him saying, **"I will always share My heart with you."**

Later, in the afternoon, I picked up the devotional *Streams in the Dessert*. I read February 1st:

> *This is my doing. (1 King 12:24)*
>
> *The disappointments of life are simply hidden appointments of love. C.A. Fox*
>
> *My child, I have a message for you today. Let me whisper it in your ear so any storm clouds that may arise will shine with glory, and the rough places you may have to walk will be made smooth...*

I wept for joy. The Lord had a message for me. It was a beautiful message that He spoke through Laura A. Barter Snow. The Lord is so precious! I love Him! And I love His hidden appointments of love. This was *His* doing.

Psalm 116:1-2 (NIV) I love the LORD, for he heard my voice...Because he turned his ear to me, I will call on him as long as I live.

Psalm 117

Cowman L.B., Streams in the Dessert (Grand Rapids: Zondervan 1997) 56

———

"Satan cannot crush a thankful Christian
unless he succeeds in robbing him
of his thankfulness."

(Journal 5-25-2010)

"Practice being misunderstood
without defending yourself or retaliating.
Find joy in it.
You are practicing for the future.
Leave your reputation in My hands."

"Love to be misunderstood;
pray for it to be made right."

December 1

(Journal 12-9-2015)
  Through a dream last night, I felt the Lord awakened me to a problem I never thought I had—jealousy. In the dream, the jealousy was manifested in a couple of other women. But when I woke from the dream, it made me wonder if those were really *my* feelings being exhibited.

  I asked the Lord if I had a problem with jealousy. The Lord brought one scene after another to my mind, and I realized that because the jealousy was so subtle, I hadn't recognized it.

  I wept and prayed this afternoon, asking the Lord to forgive me. Through tears, I reached for my *Strongest Concordance,* and flung the big heavy book open onto my drawing table. I wanted to do a Biblical word study on 'jealousy'. When I looked at the open book in front of me, I saw through my tears that it had opened to the word 'jealousy'. This was a sixteen hundred page book! If I needed confirmation that the Lord was trying to speak to me about jealousy, *this* was it!

Job 33:14-15,17 (NLT) "For God speaks again and again, though people do not recognize it. He speaks in dreams, in visions of the night, when deep sleep falls on people as they lie in their beds. He whispers in their ears and terrifies them with warnings. He makes them turn from doing wrong; he keeps them from pride."

Psalm 51:6-7

December 2

(Journal 12-10-2015)
  We can make an idol of anything that does not draw our focus to Jesus. Creation was meant to draw our focus to Jesus.

Anything beautiful should draw our focus to Jesus in praise and worship.

When we eat, we turn our focus to Jesus and give Him thanks for what He has provided. When we give thanks to the Lord for everything, we are using things rightly, letting them draw our attention to the Lord.

As I thank the Lord for the wind, right now, the wind becomes the vehicle to drive my gaze to God.

When we 'give thanks for all men' (1 Timothy 2:1), we are directing our gaze to Jesus, rather than letting any person in our life be elevated to a position God never intended for that person to have.

We don't let our minds 'set' on the things of the earth, but we let those things be a springboard to direct us up to Jesus, who is sitting at the right hand of the Father.

"Father, forgive me for having worshiped (adored) the created rather than the Creator, when the created became the object of my focus rather than the Creator."

Colossians 3:2 (NIV) Set your minds on things above, not on earthly things.

Philippians 3:19 (NIV) Their destiny is destruction, their god is their stomach, and their glory is in their shame. Their mind is [set] on earthly things.

Matthew 14:19
John 1:1-3

December 3

(Journal 12-11-2015)
About a year ago, I asked the Lord what I could eat at bedtime, and he said, **"A handful of walnuts."** Tonight, I read a news article that said a new study on walnuts revealed

that they are a good thing to eat before bed because they help you sleep. They have melatonin in them.

"Thank You, Jesus."

Isaiah 8:19b (NIV) "...should not a people inquire of their God?"

Proverbs 2:6

December 4

(Journal 12-21-2015)
"Weep and wail for the destruction that is about to come upon the earth. Weep for the inhabitants of the earth. For in My strength I will plow under those who have defied Me. I will destroy the earth with a blow from My fist. It shall be plundered and laid waste. All shall reel and wonder at their destruction. All shall face the Almighty on the day of judgement.

Many will look to Me and be glad in that day, but many will lose their lives for the destruction they have brought to the earth.

Though the light will grow dim, the barren lands will sing again. For God will not bring an end to all, but will spare a few in the land. Those who have washed their robes and made themselves right before the Lord shall sing for joy."

"Sing, little one,
Sing while the light is still here.
Sing to those whose heart can hear.
Sing of life, and light and treasure.
Sing of faith that flows beyond measure.

Make My life an offering,

That others may join you as you sing.
And take what's good and take what's wise,
And hold it out before men's eyes.

Lift up your voice and sing of life:
    'Let go of hate, let go of strife.
    Let go of that which hinders love.
    Find life, find grace from God above.

    Go on, go on and hear His cry,
    Find life, find help, before you die,
    Why faint along the way, He said,
    When in His hand He offers bread.'"

Revelation 11:18 (NIV) " The nations were angry; and your wrath has come. The time has come for judging the dead, and for rewarding your servants the prophets and your saints and those who reverence your name, both small and great—and for destroying those who destroy the earth."

Daniel 11:33-35
Daniel 12
Revelation 22:14
Joel 1:13-15
Isaiah 26:9-11

December 5

(Journal 1-2-2016)
    "Take heart, little one. Your Father is here—mighty to save. You shall uncover My love for you more and more as you look to Me for all that pertains to life. My eyes are upon you always, to draw you close, to meet your needs, to help you fall in love again.

Partake of My flesh, partake of My blood. Let Me cleanse you from all that is unworthy of My Spirit which abides in you. Restore your heart to fellowship. Restore your hands to war against the enemy of your soul. He shall not have the victory, nor gain ground you do not give him. Resist him and he will flee.

You are in need of My mercy. Throw yourself upon My love and care. Know that I am here to protect you—to deliver you from the evil one. Cast your cares on Me and I will sustain you. Find your life in Me.

You have sought rest and I have given you rest. Now seek the battle and I will give you victory. I will restore your heart to that of a warrior. Let My Spirit be made manifest in you. Let My power be strong on your behalf. I am here—mighty to save. You are in need of My help. Stand firm against the enemy of your soul. Resist the devil and he will flee from you. You shall be crowned in victory. As you lay down your life for Me, you shall be delivered. Though the enemy has set a snare for your soul, he shall not gain the upper hand. I shall defeat him by the power of the blood."

1 Corinthians 15:57 (NIV) But thanks be to God! He gives us the victory through our Lord Jesus Christ.

John 6:32-58
Revelation 12:10-12

December 6

(Journal 1-16-2016)
"Learn to listen, little one. Let your ears be unstopped. Pay attention to the voice that speaks in your heart. I'm here. I'm with you, an ever present help in trouble. Do not neglect Me while you go about

your day as if I don't exist. Speak to Me. Speak with Me. Let your thoughts and prayers be directed at Me. I am your best friend. Do not neglect this friendship. I am here, mighty to save, ready to save you from the cares of this life. I am here. Hear My voice."

Ezekiel 3:10 (NIV) And he said to me, "Son of man, listen carefully and take to heart all the words I speak to you."

Isaiah 63:1 (NIV) Who is this coming from Edom, from Bozrah, with his garments stained crimson? Who is this, robed in splendor, striding forward in the greatness of his strength? "It is I, speaking in righteousness, mighty to save."

Psalm 46:1 (NIV) God is our refuge and strength, an ever-present help in trouble.

December 7

(Journal 1-17-2016)
"In My life is light; light to light the way ahead. Choose life. Choose light. Choose joy in My presence. Clasp your hand in Mine and enjoy the sweet fellowship that is yours for the taking.
I have laid out a path for you, little one. Follow it with all your heart. Let your soul be unburdened by My nearness and My love. Stretch out your hand and find healing. Know the joys of My fellowship with you. I will strengthen you and give you peace. Partake of My love, partake of My life. Grasp My hand in yours and walk with Me. My presence is so real for those who spend time with Me. Delight yourself in the abundance of peace. Your Father is pleased to give you the kingdom. You have tasted a foretaste of things to come." (I feel His smile and His delight.)

"I love You, Jesus."

Daniel 7:18 (NIV) "But the saints of the Most High will receive the kingdom and will possess it forever—yes, for ever and ever."

Luke 12:32
Romans 14:17

December 8

(Journal 2-4-2016)
"I love You, Jesus. Sweet peace engulfs me.
Today was a delightful day in Your presence."

"Let your heart register 'full' as you spend time with Me. You will notice more opportunities for your heart to register 'full' as you spend more time in My presence. Your days will be spent in joy and delight as you delight in Me.

I love you, My child. What you feel is My love being poured out on and through you. Energy comes from spending time with Me. Joy comes from the laughter welling up in your soul.

Know that I am pleased with you, little one."

"Thank You, Jesus."

Psalm 68:3 (NIV) But may the righteous be glad and rejoice before God; may they be happy and joyful.

Psalm 97:11-12

December 9

(Journal 3-9-2016)

"Let truth be your rear guard. Stayed upon Me, hearts are fully blessed. Do not fear. Know that I am with you. As the enemy seeks to let loose his destructive force upon your lives, know that My power is greater than all of the power of his hordes put together. You are protected, little one. I have My hands upon you to cover you—to hide you from the enemy's onslaught. Your life is in My hands. He cannot affect you except that I allow him free rein. Trust Me; trust that I have your good in mind."

Isaiah 58:8 (NIV) " Then your light will break forth like the dawn, and your healing will quickly appear; then your righteousness will go before you, and *the glory of the LORD will be your rear guard."* (God protects our back too.)

Psalm 3:3

December 10

(Journal 4-24-2016)

"Blessed is he who walks by the power of My Spirit. He shall rejoice in the shadow of My wings.

Learn to rest in Me when trouble prevails. This lesson has been long in coming, but it is something you must go through to make you strong. In Me is strength. If you rest in Me you shall not want for strength. Stay true, stay calm. Rest in Me.

I love you, little one. The joys of My fellowship are reserved for you because you have chosen to know Me and to make Me known.

Dig deep, little one. Dig deeper still. Rest on My promises, trust in My love.

Know the character and heart of God and you shall never want for peace."

Psalm 145:13 (NLT) For your kingdom is an everlasting kingdom. You rule throughout all generations. The LORD always keeps his promises; he is gracious in all he does.

1 Chronicles 16:8-9
Philippians 3:10

December 11

(Journal 5-4-2016)

"Let your heart meld with mine. Clasp your hand in mine. Focus on what is important to Me as I train you to hear My voice and My heart. Let My Spirit influence you in all things. I am here to partner with you in everything. Don't leave My Spirit untapped as you go about your day as if I don't exist. Cling to Me. Look to Me in everything.

You shall grow more and more used to lifting everything up to Me for My consideration and purpose. Train yourself to hear My voice. Train yourself to hear My heart. Never leave this resource untapped. Draw from Me all that you need for life and godliness. You cannot exhaust My supply. You often leave it untapped when I would have you use Me.

Know Me, little one. Know Me so well that you do not question My love. Though you must always test the spirit behind the message—trust Me, when once you know it is I, your Lord and Savior, master, speaking to you.

Be diligent in listening and discerning My voice."

1 John 4:1-3
John 16:12-13
John 10:27

December 12

(Journal 5-25-2016)

I woke up this morning with a phrase running through my mind on a repetitive note. I felt disturbed by the repetition, having put up with it for too long. I finally asked, "Lord, what is causing this repetition? I'm taking vitamins!" He answered, **"It's a spirit of confusion."** I asked Him what caused it, and He said, **"It came from saying, 'I don't know what to do', 'I don't know what to do'."**

We can give way to a spirit of confusion, just like we give way to a spirit of fear, or a spirit of worry and anxiety.

I am so thankful to the Lord for showing me this. It is really a lack of trust in the Lord. I should *never* say, "I don't know what to do," but should *always* turn to the Lord in prayer and seek *His* direction and guidance.

I suppose, "I don't know what to wear!" falls into the same category. It certainly produces a feeling of confusion, stress and anxiety.

I just thought of another door to confusion, "I don't know what to eat." This is said in an attempt to avoid the foods that affect me, but it is really giving in to self-pity.

"Oh, Lord, forgive me for my Godless living."

This is why the Lord says, "Be anxious for nothing, but in everything, by prayer and supplication, with thanksgiving, let your requests be made known to God, and the peace of God, which surpasses all understanding, will guard your hearts and minds through Christ Jesus" (Philippians 4:6, 7 NKJV). When we give way to anxiety, we open the door to the enemy.

Isaiah 28:26 (NIV) His God instructs him and teaches him the right way.

December 13

(Journal 6-14-2016)

"Find in Me your strength. Let Me be strong on your behalf. I would uphold you by My mighty right hand. Do not fear the darkness, do not flee the shadows. Stand strong, stand firm.

When your heart is lonely, look to Me. When life feels overwhelming, look to Me. I will be your help. I am your strong tower. Rest in Me, find delight in me. When the flood waters rise, I will be your safety. When life feels tumultuous, I will be your sure landing.

Beauty stems from the heart that has weathered a storm and survived by My grace. My heart is kind toward you.

Seek My peace and pursue it. Expect My love and walk through it."

Psalm 23:4 (NIV) Even though I walk through the valley of the shadow of death, I will fear no evil, for you are with me; your rod and your staff, they comfort me.

Psalm 124

December 14

(Journal 6-25-2016)
I went to meet with the Lord at 2:30 in the morning, because my heart was grieved with my neglect of Him.

"Look to Me, little one. I long to share with you so much, but you have left me to the back corner of your life. When you do not take the time to listen, you neglect so great a comfort—you leave off so large a smile.

Feel My love, little one. Feel My joy.

Learn to trust Me. Learn to know Me. All of life is full of searching, but few find a life that is full of finding. You have that ability to 'find'; use it well."

"Please forgive me, Father, for not taking the time to listen. I am ashamed that I let myself feel too busy to remember to spend time in the greatest relationship in heaven or on earth.

You have been so kind to speak to my heart.

Thank You for so great a relationship. Thank You for so great a love."

"Grow in grace, little one, grow in love. Yield yourself up to Me, to use you as I will."

Jeremiah 29:13 (NIV) "You will seek me and find me when you seek me with all your heart."

Psalm 22:26
2 Chronicles 15:1-15

December 15

(Journal 6-28-2016)
 Yesterday, the Lord performed a miracle of healing for me. This morning, while praying, its lesson became very clear: "Freely you have received; freely give" (Matt. 10:8b, NIV).

 The Lord healed what should have been a bad burn. I, for some reason, patted my hand twice on the bottom of a frying pan that had been sitting on a burner at medium-high heat for about fifteen minutes. I had forgotten the heat was on. I screamed and dropped the frying pan onto the vinyl-covered kitchen table, then lifted the frying pan instantly, realizing what a mistake I had made. The frying pan had melted a huge hole in the table cloth. As I rushed to get my hand under water at the sink, I thought, *"This is not good. This is a bad burn."* John came into the kitchen when he heard me scream. I had one hand in the running water and the other holding up the hot frying pan. He found a container for me to soak my hand in.

 I peered at my fingers through the water and wondered if I had lost my finger prints. There were red/white ovals on each seared finger. John looked at my fingers and said, "That's a bad burn; that's going to hurt for days." He gave me two Tylenol and instructed me to not cover my fingers.

 Right away, I asked John to pray, and I prayed also. I told the Lord that I was his servant–that I would like to be able to use my fingers, but if He wanted his servant to have burned fingers, that was up to Him.

 I felt the healing process as it was happening; I also watched it. My fingers started to feel soft instead of hard. The color changed until it looked normal. About twenty minutes later, I could not tell I had been burned. One of the girls looked at my fingers and asked where the burn was. Remarkably, it was no longer discernable. John was surprised when he saw what had happened.

 There was no pain, hardness, swelling or blistering as an after-effect. "Thank You, Jesus."

 I hope that the right hand I use to touch others for healing will remind me, "Freely you have received; freely give."

Psalm 40:5a (NLT) O Lord my God, you have performed many wonders for us.

Psalm 77:14
Acts 14:3
1 Corinthians 12:7-11

December 16

(Journal 7-12-2016)
"Take great delight in Me, little one, for I delight in you.

Long to spend time in My presence. Long to serve Me with all of your heart. True longing is based upon true loving.

You do not know, little one, the strength and the love and the joy and the courage that come from spending time with Me. If you truly understood how much comes from Me, you would not neglect this time. Your 'life' would depend on it. Don't run on 'empty'. Take in My power. Take in My life. Find joy. Find strength. Find life. Find fulfillment in Me."

I took time listening to the Lord's Spirit and praising Him—delighting in Him.

Ephesians 6:10 (NLT) A final word: Be strong in the Lord and in his mighty power.

Ephesians 3:14-20
Isaiah 40:29

December 17

(Journal 8-14-2016)
"Grow in grace, little one. I do not just ask you to have grace for others, but I ask you to have grace for yourself. Do not fling accusations at yourself any more than I would have you fling accusations at others. Do not be a mouthpiece for the enemy—even in your heart.

I love you, and My heart is for you, not against you. When you are against yourself, you live with a divided heart—the Holy Spirit against the flesh—the enemy of your souls.

Live to please Me, not yourself. Live to encourage others, and allow Me, the Holy Spirit, to encourage your heart. Live in the fullness of Christ.

Do not grieve My Holy Spirit by your self-talk. Do not stand against the truths of My word as you mingle with the enemy's thoughts. Yes, you have been working with the enemy, but you do not need to work hand in hand with the enemy of your soul.

Live with kingdom thoughts. Live with kingdom truths. Say 'No' to the enemy of your soul. Do not believe his lies, but stand against them. Live to bless, live to love. Live to strengthen the brotherhood of believers. If your focus is on yourself, it is off of Me.

Take heart, little one. If I be *for* you, who can be against you? The enemy's plans will fail as you trust in Me."

"Lord, I feel so unworthy of You—but I am *more* than a conqueror through Christ who loves me" (*Romans 8:37*).

"My soul is tired, but I can do all things through Christ who gives me strength" (*Philippians 4:13*).

"I have no love on my own, but God has given me everything that pertains unto life and godliness" (*2 Peter 1:3*).

2 Corinthians 10:5 (NIV) We demolish arguments and every pretension that sets itself up against the knowledge of God, and we take captive every thought to make it obedient to Christ.

2 Corinthians 5:15
Revelation 12:9-10

———◆———

December 18

(Journal 8-3-2016)
    "Good for you, little one, coming to hear My heart. Place your life before Me, into My hands. Let Me bring beauty into your soul, light into your countenance, and joy in your demeanor. Soak in My presence. Know so great a love." (*Weeping…His presence is felt.*)

    "Thank You for Your beauty, Lord. Thank You for Your touch."

    "Let My Spirit feed you. Find your nourishment in Me.
    Don't lose touch with Me, little one."

    "Forgive me for the times I have been 'disconnected' from You, Father.
    You are my joy and delight. I am amazed at how You love me."

John 6:35 (NIV) Then Jesus declared, "I am the bread of life. He who comes to me will never go hungry, and he who believes in me will never be thirsty."

Psalm 19:8 (NIV) The precepts of the LORD are right, giving joy to the heart. The commands of the LORD are radiant, giving light to the eyes.

Psalm 97:11-12

December 19

(Journal 8-5-2016)

"You can strive and work and struggle, but you will learn that all you really need to do is rest in Me. In Me, your strivings cease. *I* empower you to live the Christian life. *I* pour out My love into your hearts. *I* give you the desire to live a godly life, and *I* give you the power to accomplish it.

Yes, I know you forget, and that is why I tell you so often, 'Rest in Me'."

"Lord, help me to live a life of resting in You."

"I long to fill you, little one; I long to fill you *full* of My power, My joy, My strength, My love; but you have gone your own way. You have not completely surrendered your life to me in actions, but only in words. Oh, little one, learn to live in My presence. Learn to trust Me for everything. I will fulfill you beyond anything you can imagine."

Ephesians 3:20 (NIV) Now to him who is able to do immeasurably more than all we ask or imagine, according to his power that is at work within us,...

2 Thessalonians 1:11 (NLT) So we keep on praying for you, asking our God to enable you to live a life worthy of his call.

May he give you the power to accomplish all the good things your faith prompts you to do.

Colossians 1:29 (NIV) To this end I labor, struggling with all *His energy, which so powerfully works in me.*

———————

December 20

(Journal 8-30-2016)

Every spider, every cricket, every millipede, etc., is a call to spiritual warfare. Every time I spot one of these, it's a call to pray, or speak in the name of Jesus against the enemy of our souls, of our church, of the saints—our children included.

Perhaps bugs will have some benefit in our house after all.

Luke 10:17-20 (NIV) The seventy-two returned with joy and said, "Lord, even the demons submit to us in your name." He replied, "I saw Satan fall like lightning from heaven. I have given you authority to trample on snakes and scorpions and to overcome all the power of the enemy; nothing will harm you. However, do not rejoice that the spirits submit to you, but rejoice that your names are written in heaven."

Note: Amazingly, as I started to use spiders and bugs as a reminder to pray, I also started noticing a greatly diminished supply of them.

———————

December 21

(Journal 9-14-2016)
"Draw near, little one, draw near. Let Me hold you as you rest in My love. Know the healing balm of My touch upon your heart. Let peace soak into your entire being. Oh, the joys set before you—oh, the peace.

Clasp your hand in Mine, little one. Know the strength and support of One who loves you. My love blossoms in the heart that is focused on Me. That is where a healthy heart comes from.

Let My peace enfold you. Bask in Me. Delight in Me."

John 16:33 (NIV) "I have told you these things, so that in me you may have peace. In this world you will have trouble. But take heart! I have overcome the world."

Jude 1:1-2
Psalm 29:11

December 22

(Journal 11-8-2016)
The Lord gave me a dream that left a lasting impression. In the dream, a strong wind was driving me up against the inside wall of a second story house. It forced me up against a window. As I pictured the glass breaking, I said, "Lord, I trust You." I knew that whatever happened, I could trust Him. I felt such a peace in that trust.

Sure enough, the glass burst and the wind carried me on my back out the window. Again, I said, "Lord, I trust You." I felt completely abandoned into His care, as the wind current took me all around the yard. It was an exhilarating feeling to be carried on the wind. Again I said, "Lord, I trust You." I did not know where I would go, and I was not thinking about the outcome, I simply trusted Him.

In the dream, I did not know how or where I landed, but I found myself telling others about my experience, and how I had trusted the Lord.

In real life, I shared this dream with our Wednesday night prayer group. I found I was telling it to some of the same people I had been sharing with in my dream. I realized that the Lord wanted this dream to encourage others as well.

What did the Lord want from the Israelites when He led them from Egypt into the wilderness? He wanted to hear, "Lord, we trust You; we don't have food or water, but we trust You. Please provide us what we need. Thank You."

Deuteronomy 1:31-33 (NIV) "...and in the desert. There you saw how the LORD your God carried you, as a father carries his son, all the way you went until you reached this place. In spite of this, *you did not trust in the LORD your God,* who went ahead of you on your journey, in fire by night and in a cloud by day, to search out places for you to camp and to show you the way you should go."

Nahum 1:7 (NIV) The LORD is good, a refuge in times of trouble. He cares for those who trust in him,

Isaiah 12:2-3

December 23

(Journal 1-28-2017)
"Let My life fill you as you spend time with Me. Let My light flood your soul. Sense My cleansing as you spend time in My presence. Delight in Me as I restore your soul.

I love you, little one. Feel bathed in My love. In Me there is hope. In Me there is joy. I dispense all of these to you as you spend time with Me. Be encouraged. Be strengthened. Find life, find peace. Let My life fill you, little one, to overflowing. Those who experience abundant life have spent time receiving from Me. In Me is abundance. In Me is life. Take, eat, enjoy. Don't go away empty. Don't leave before you are full."

"Lord, I receive Your life. I receive Your abundance."

I rose from this time with the Lord, refreshed, energized, and full of joy as I prepared for a visitor.

John 10:10 (HCSB) "A thief comes only to steal and to kill and to destroy. I have come so that they may have life and have it in abundance."

John 1:4
1 John 5:11-12

December 24

(Journal 2-8-2017)
"Ah, little one, do you understand that spending time with Me brings health to your body, mind and spirit? Do you understand that resting in My presence brings you peace? Then why do you leave off so great a joy? Why do you forsake so great a pleasure? Have you let the enemy convince you that time with Me is a New Age endeavor? Have you let his poison seep in between us? Open your ears. Open your heart. Rejoice in the One who loves you."

"Forgive Me, Father. I love this time with You."

2 Corinthians 11:3 (NIV) But I am afraid that just as Eve was deceived by the serpent's cunning, your minds may somehow be led astray from your sincere and pure devotion to Christ.

Isaiah 9:6
Psalm 85:8-10

December 25

(Journal 4-12-2017)
　　With tears spilling out of my eyes, I thanked the Lord for the book *'Touch the World through Prayer'* by Wesley L. Duewel. He reminded me in my spirit, **"If you ever feel dry in prayer, use a book on prayer to prime the pump of prayer again."**

Romans 12:12
Ephesians 6:18
1 Timothy 2:1

December 26

(Journal 4-19-2017)
　　Our garden reminds me to pray: "Lord, bless the growth of this church. Help us to grow more in love with Jesus and each other. Help us to grow closer to You. Help us to grow in the power of Your Spirit, in holiness and in godliness. Help us to grow in the knowledge of the truth. Help us to grow up in Christ to a greater level of maturity. Help us to grow in the use of the gifts. Help us to grow in influence, in the community and in the world. Help us to grow in understanding and

insight concerning the word of God. Help us to grow in awareness of each other's needs, and in the needs of the poor around us. Help us to grow in favor with God and man. Help us to grow in our appreciation of others."

Isaiah 61:11 (NIV) For as the soil makes the sprout come up and a garden causes seeds to grow, so the Sovereign LORD will make righteousness and praise spring up before all nations.

Luke 2:52 (NIV) And Jesus grew in wisdom and stature, and in favor with God and men.

2 Corinthians 13:9
Colossians 4:12

———————

December 27

(Journal 5-10-2017)

"Warm yourself up to My heart, little one. Rejoice in My presence—I am mighty to save.

Your cares have been many lately; lay them at My feet. Know that I care for you more than you care for yourself, more than you care for those around you. You only prove that you know this when you give Me everything.

Yes, little one, find rest in Me. Find strength, find joy. Your heart has been heavy because you have not been coming to Me. I will lift your burdens, even if you feel they are of your own making. I care that your heart is light and happy, for then you can serve Me with joy.

Follow through with the things that I have told you. Hear My heart and obey. As you walk in obedience I will share more and more with you. The heart and flesh are weak, but the Spirit is willing. Walk in the Spirit and you will not fulfill the desires

of the flesh. Don't follow the dictates of the body; follow the dictates of the Spirit. Live to please Me, not yourself."

Psalm 68:19 (NIV) Praise be to the Lord, to God our Savior, who daily bears our burdens.

Psalm 100:2 (NIV) Worship the LORD with gladness; come before him with joyful songs.

Romans 6:16
Ephesians 5:10

December 28

(Journal 6-7-2017)
    I have enjoyed watching the birds at the bird bath outside our kitchen window whenever I wash the dishes. Tonight I thought, "I'm watching and enjoying the birds, but I'm not praying." The idea came, to pray for a person whenever a bird came to the bath. I prayed for one friend and then another. I remembered to pray for my childhood friend, Alice, who had long beautiful hair, matching the color of a robin's red breast. A blackbird reminded me to pray for a person who needed salvation.
    As I prayed in the living room afterward, the Lord said, **"You will be a prayer warrior again."** What a joy! Suddenly the phone rang, and it was one of the people for whom I had just fervently prayed. I told the woman, "I was just praying for you!" She seemed delighted.
    Today was a day of prayer and fasting. The Lord often gives me good ideas about how to be closer to Him on days when I am fasting.

1 Thessalonians 5:25
2 Thessalonians 3:1-2

Ephesians 6:19-20
2 Corinthians 1:11

December 29

(Journal 6-13-2017)

"When life is at its darkest moment, trust Me. When life is full of light and joy and laughter, trust Me. Look to Me always. Know that I am here. Know that My hand is upon you. I will not leave you alone. Even the dark is not dark to those who hold My hand. Trust Me through all of life's struggles. Trust Me through all of life's pain, and life will hold so much joy for you that you will not be able to contain it. Let Me deliver you from the evil one. Let Me restore your heart to peace in every situation. Come to Me. Rest in Me. Wait with expectation to hear My voice. Let Me shelter you in My love. Grow still. Grow calm. Let the anxieties of life melt away. Release your fears and your tears into My loving hands. I will take them from you. You do not need to bear the load that is too heavy for the human heart."

Psalm 139:11-12
Psalm 56:3
Psalm 34:4

December 30

(Journal 9-5-2017)

"Oh, little one, to you does My heart call, to you do I reach out in love. Find time to sit in My presence.

Find time to kneel at My feet. I offer you My life. I offer you a wealth of treasure beyond understanding. I offer you wisdom and knowledge, love, joy and peace beyond anything you can imagine. These are all yours.

Oh, little one, do not neglect your time with Me. If you have to leave other things undone—come. You have lost so much because of your negligence. I have so much to give you, yet you seem satisfied with the crumbs. Do not disdain My word. Do not disdain My calling. I have called and beckoned and wooed, yet you seldom come. *Now* is the time to be revived. *Now* is the time to cling to Me with all your heart. *Now* you will receive victory if you heed My words and do not neglect your time with Me. I love you, little one, but you have needed strong words to steer your heart into My presence."

"Please forgive me, Father. I know You have so much planned and I don't want to hinder Your plans by constantly giving in to the flesh—or going my own way. I long to be used by You.

I have wanted to spend time with You and enjoy You forever. What hinders me, Lord?"

"Fear of the unknown; fear of what you might have to do."

"It's true, Lord. I have had fear of the unknown. I have had fear of what You might call me to do. I have been living in fear for too long."

"Oh, Lord, give me courage. Help me to live a life of victory. Forgive me, Father. Oh, Jesus, would You wash me anew in the blood of Jesus. Cleanse me from the sin of fear—lack of trust."

"Lord, help me to go from strength to strength."

"Let My love overflow within you, little one."

"Revive my heart, Father. Revive my heart."

(A song comes to mind, *The Steadfast Love of the Lord*, written by Edith McNeill.)

It's amazing to think that we are the ones who determine whether or not we will live a victorious life. It is not God's fault if we do not reach the purposes and plans that God has for our lives.

Psalm 62

December 31

(Journal 9-6-2017)
"Live a life of love, little one. Seek to make My influence felt in many circles. Bring My love and hope to the hurting. Bring My care to the downcast. Bring My rest to the downtrodden."

Ephesians 5:1-2 (NLT) Imitate God, therefore, in everything you do, because you are his dear children. Live a life filled with love, following the example of Christ. He loved us and offered himself as a sacrifice for us, a pleasing aroma to God.

Conclusion

There are some who will read this devotional with a critical eye, looking for fault. They will miss the heart of it. They will miss the Holy Spirit wooing them unto Himself, calling for them to spend time in His presence.

There are some who will say, "God doesn't speak like that to us today. We have the scriptures; if another voice speaks, it is Satan." To that I say, I'm sorry that you are missing out on so great a joy, so great a comfort. I am sorry that you are missing out on so much encouragement, instruction and guidance. How is it you believe that Satan can speak to us today, but God is mute, silent—zip? Is the God of the universe not much more powerful than Satan?

There are some who talk about the 'presence' of God as though it were a thing to be disdained—a 'New Age' term and idea. The whole Bible is replete with the presence of God from beginning to end. His presence is found, not only through stories and illustrations, but in the very act of His Spirit speaking through the prophets to record scripture. Moses said to God, in Exodus 33:16, "How will anyone know that you look favorably on me—on me and your people—if you don't go with us? For *your presence* among us sets your people and me apart from all other people on the earth."

There are some who have a form of godliness, but deny the power—the Holy Spirit, and all His gifts. They do not believe certain gifts are for today. By denying these gifts and proclaiming that those who use them are doing so by the power of Satan, they are setting themselves in the camp of those who commit the unpardonable sin (Matthew 12:32). Run from that attitude as though your very life depends on it, for it does.

We are told in scripture not to despise prophesying (1 Thessalonians 5:20). Prophecy is listening to God and communicating a message from Him. Paul's message to the church today is for us to "eagerly desire spiritual gifts, especially the gift of prophecy" (1 Corinthians 14:1). Revelation 19:10 says, "For the testimony of Jesus is the spirit of prophecy." Yes, test the prophecy. Is it leading you toward sin and away from God and scripture? Or is it leading you *toward* God, *toward* holiness, *toward* obedience, *toward* scripture?

There are others, who will read what I have written, and say, "If God can speak to her, then He can speak to me also." They will want to say, "Speak, Lord, for your servant is listening" (*1 Samuel 3:9*). And they will discover a relationship so beautiful that they will *never* doubt the existence of God. They will look forward to spending time with Jesus for all of eternity.

But this beautiful relationship is only for those who have given their lives to Jesus. It is only for those who have asked Him to come into their hearts to be their Lord and Savior (*John 1:12*). It is for those who repent of their sins and desire to turn away from all ungodliness and follow Jesus. It is for those who desire to be filled with the Holy Spirit.

Jesus shed His blood on the cross to cover our sins and to make us holy. He now offers us the free gift of salvation because He already took upon himself the punishment that our sins deserved. That's how much He loved us.

For those of you who desire to repent of your sins by turning from them and accepting the free gift of salvation that God offers, you can pray something like this:

"Lord Jesus, I know that I am a sinner and have strayed from Your paths of righteousness. There is nothing I can do to save myself. I receive You, and accept Your free gift of salvation. Would You forgive me for my sins and give me a new heart and life? Would You come in and fill me with Your Holy Spirit? Would You lead, guide and instruct me for the rest of my life, and be my *Lord* as well as my Savior? Thank You for saving me from my sin and turning my heart toward love, purity, godliness, holiness and truth. Help me to understand the scriptures as I read. Train me through them, that I might follow You with all of my heart. Help me to love You with all of my heart, soul, mind and strength, and to love others, by the power of Your Holy Spirit. Grow Your fruit of righteousness in me (*Galatians 5:22-23*) as I walk in Your Spirit."

If, after praying this prayer, you find that nothing has changed, you do not feel any different, and life goes on as it is, then d o not fool yourself into thinking that you have become a child of God and have received the Holy Spirit. Do not think that you just need to 'accept by faith' that God has come in and made you a child of God. When the Holy Spirit comes in, you will *know* it (*Romans 8:16*). If you have any doubts, then you may n ot have been born again into a new life. God may still require something of you. Find out what it is. Seek Him with all your r heart.

Some people have a personality that is strong and independent. They cannot quite give God everything. They want to maintain control. They don't trust Him to have their best in mind. When they can give God everything, they will find the exciting relationship they are missing. They will *know* they are a child of God. They will *know* He has filled them with His Spirit.

Churches are full of people who have mouthed the words, "Jesus, come into my heart," but they do not exhibit a changed life. They do not love the scriptures. They do not love the children of God, though they might act like it. They do not have the power of God in their lives, identified by His gifts. They do not have a strong desire to witness. They do not yet have a love for godliness and a hatred of sin in themselves. They do not have an underlying peace. This is because their lives have not yet been transformed by the Holy Spirit. They have not yet been born again into the kingdom of God.

May the life of Christ fill you to overflowing.

In His love,
Laura Kringle

laurakringle87@gmail.com

Made in the USA
Monee, IL
30 April 2023

32656391R00167